Healthy Heart, Healthy Planet

Delicious Plant-Based Recipes and Tips to Reduce Heart Disease, Lose Weight, and Preserve the Environment

Dr. Cathi Misquitta  Dr. Rajiv Misquitta

ISBN: 150066488X
ISBN 13: 9781500664886
Library of Congress Control Number: 2014913497
CreateSpace Independent Publishing Platform
North Charleston, South Carolina
Photography by Brian Tokuyoshi

For all our families, who believed in us.

For my father, Reginald Misquitta, who struggled
with heart disease. He had the courage to follow this path
and also encouraged me to tell others about his story.

For my mother, Maria Misquitta,
who taught me that anything is possible.

Authors' Note

The information in this book is not meant to replace medical therapy. Please discuss any medical conditions and questions that you may have with your physician.

It's also important to obtain medical advice before engaging in any major change to your diet or exercise program. Your physician can be your best ally. Feel free to share this book with him or her.

It is our sincere hope that you will experience the benefits of a healthy lifestyle just as we have.

To your good health,

Cathi and Rajiv Misquitta

Contents

Chapter 1 - **Dr. Rajiv Misquitta's Advice on Preventing and Reversing Heart Disease** 1

Section 1 *A Harrowing Tale of Heart Disease* 3

Section 2 *Heart Disease: Prevalence and Causes* 6

Section 3 *Evidence for a Low-Fat, Vegan Diet to Reduce Heart Disease* 7

Section 4 *Heart Disease: The Need for Change* 10

Section 5 *Other Dietary Considerations* 11

Section 6 *My Father: A Case in Point* 15

Section 7 *Tips for Adopting a Low-Fat, Vegan Diet* 16

Section 8 *Weight Loss* 17

Section 9 *Yoga* 18

Section 10 *Exercise* 20

Chapter 2 - **Tips from Cathi's Kitchen** 21

Planet-friendly Benefits of a Vegetarian Diet 23

Section 1 *Grocery Shopping: Menus and Shopping Lists* 24

Section 2 *Reading Nutrition Labels* 30

Section 3 *Preparing Food From Bulk* 30

Section 4 *Cooking Without Fat and Preparing Meatless Meals* 31

Chapter 3 - **Breakfast ideas** 33

Planet-friendly Benefits of a Vegetarian Diet 35

Chapter 4 - **Salads** 53

Five Simple Tips to Reducing Kitchen Waste 55

Chapter 5 - **Soups** 69
    Add Fresh Fruits and Vegetables to Your Diet and Your Life 71

Chapter 6 - **Main Dishes** 85
    Solar Cooking 87
    Section 1 *Tortillas, Sandwiches, and Wraps* 89
    Section 2 *Grains*.. 113
    Section 3 *Potatoes and Vegetables*.. 123
    Section 4 *Pasta* 135

Chapter 7 - **Side Dishes** 143
    Ditch the Car 145

Chapter 8 - **Dressings and Sauces** 161
    Keeping it Clean and Green 163

Index 173

Endnotes 179

Dr. Rajiv Misquitta's Advice on Preventing and Reversing Heart Disease

Section 1 *A Harrowing Tale of Heart Disease*

It was a brisk November morning in 2008, three days before my older son's fourth birthday. Bare trees lined the streets. I dropped my boys off at school and headed for work. I had just turned forty, and life was good. I had a busy medical practice, a wonderful wife, and two sons: Callister and Griffin. Halfway into my twenty-minute commute, I became nauseated and felt intense discomfort in the pit of my stomach. Could this be the Chinese food that I ate last night? Maybe I drank too much coffee. The discomfort magnified, and I was glad to stop at a red light.

I started to feel worse as the light turned green. It became difficult to catch my breath, and then pain exploded on the left side of my chest. Memories of my father suffering a heart attack flashed through my head, and I knew I was in trouble. I was now only five minutes from the hospital. Foolishly, I stepped on the gas and barely made it into the parking lot. I put my head down on the steering wheel and steeled myself for the long trek to the emergency room. It was the longest five minutes of my life. I stumbled into the hospital and tapped on my friend's shoulder, an emergency room physician who was about to change his shift. "I think that I am having a heart attack," I said.

He quickly placed me on a stretcher. Nurses tore off my shirt and placed EKG leads on my chest and arms. After the EKG was done, I asked to see it. When the nurse brought it over, I knew that my worst nightmare was confirmed. I was having a heart attack. Many thoughts raced through my mind. How could this be happening to me? What about my family? My kids were so small.

The hospital staff reacted quickly. The nurses gave me aspirin and intravenous nitroglycerin. They drew blood and sent it to the lab. I asked for a phone so that I could call my wife at work. I could barely speak, but I managed to tell her that I was in the emergency room having a heart attack. There was silence at the other end of the line as she registered my news. She replied that she would be right over. Blood tests confirmed that I was having a heart attack, and I was prepared for a procedure called a cardiac catheterization.

As I lay on my back on a table in the cold cardiac catheterization lab, I stared up at video monitors lining one side of the wall. A cardiologist inserted a catheter into a vein in my left groin and injected dye into my coronary arteries. He determined that a main coronary artery was completely blocked, and he deployed two stents. These are hollow, cylindrical structures that open up the arteries, reestablishing blood flow to the heart. He showed me a photograph of his work when he had finished, and I was transferred to a hospital room to recover. That night a sandbag was wedged against my groin to reduce any bleeding from the catheterization site. It felt like someone was pushing a very heavy weight against my groin. The pressure was almost unbearable. Fortunately, I got through the night. The sandbag was removed the next day. After two days in the hospital, my wife took me home. I felt greatly embarrassed to be wheeled to the front entrance of the hospital and to have a nursing assistant help me into the car. Hard to believe I had been snowboarding not too long before this.

I recovered from this setback and returned to work with determination that from now on things were going to change. My cholesterol level prior to my heart attack was not too bad. My most recent low density lipoprotein (LDL) cholesterol was 128, which was considered normal. After my heart attack, I switched to a mostly vegetarian diet, but I still ate fish and nuts and used olive oil in my salads. I also joined a gym and retained a personal trainer. I started working out five times a week for forty-five minutes each session. I followed all the recommendations of my doctors and forged ahead.

Running on a treadmill four months later, on a Friday morning, I felt chest pressure build up. I slowed down to a walk, and the pressure dissipated. I increased the speed and noticed the chest pressure return. It went away when I slowed down again. Knowing this was not a good sign, I called my cardiologist. An exercise treadmill test was scheduled, which replicated what I had done at the gym but included being connected to an EKG. I felt chest pressure during the test, and when it was done I asked to see the results. With a sickening feeling, I realized that it was positive, meaning I was at great risk for having another heart attack. The report was delivered to my cardiologist, who scheduled another test the following Monday to explore this further.

On the Sunday before my next test was scheduled, I felt chest pressure at rest, which was a very bad sign. I alerted my family and called 911. A fire truck and ambulance were at my house in four minutes. The paramedics put me on a stretcher and wheeled me into the ambulance. I did not want to alarm my little boys, so I refrained from alerting them to my situation. My wife tried to distract them by showing them the fire truck. As I lay in the ambulance listening to the sounds around me, I couldn't believe this was happening again. Once again, I was wheeled into the cold cardiac catheterization room and placed on a table. The cardiologist gave me some medicine to calm me down, and I dozed a little. I awoke when the procedure was done.

The cardiologist, nationally renowned in his field, walked over to me and said, "You have an extensive amount of disease in your coronary arteries, and you need bypass surgery." He introduced me to the best cardiothoracic surgeon in town, who scheduled me for surgery a few days later, as my body needed to clear the effects of the drugs given to me during the catheterization procedure. I was shocked that I needed surgery, an outcome for which I was not mentally prepared.

I was transferred to a monitoring unit in the hospital. My family came to visit me over the weekend, and my boys jumped on my bed to lie next to me. It was hard for them to under-stand what was happening. I had a hard time controlling the tears when I looked at them, but I held them close. My wife was very supportive.

The next two days were spent waiting in the hospital. The evening before the surgery, two nurses came up to my room and shaved my chest and my legs in preparation for surgery. I felt like a sacrificial lamb being prepared for the event. Fortunately their sense of humor kept me going. That night, as I lay in my hospital room, I could hear the sounds in the street and wondered if I would make it through. The next morning I was mercifully given a sedative and wheeled to the operating room filled with nine or ten people. I was placed on my back on a thin table with narrow perpendicular arms that created the shape of a cross. My hands were fastened to each cross-section to expose my chest. The anesthesiologist leaned over me, and then the lights went out.

I awoke gasping for breath, only to find that I had a breathing tube coming out of my mouth. I felt as if I had just arisen out of the water after a long dive. The doctor encouraged me to breathe, and the tube was slowly removed from my mouth. To my horror, I also had four tubes coming out of my chest. I begged the nurse to take them out, but fortunately he did not comply. Although they were tremendously painful, they were needed to drain the fluids from my body. The next day I was moved to a step-down unit, and the chest tubes were taken out. I was encouraged to get up and walk, both of which caused excruciating pain in my chest. I was given a small pillow with a heart embroidered on it so that I could hold it close to my chest to reduce the pain caused by each move I made. I had to use a walker to move around the ward, a devastating blow to an active forty-year-old.

Determined to prevent this from happening again, and with the support of my family, I began the recovery process. I sought out all the research related to the treatment and prevention of heart disease. In the next section, I will lead you through my journey.

Section 2 *Heart Disease: Prevalence and Causes*

The leading cause of death in America and the rest of the world is heart disease, which results in almost 600,000 deaths a year.[i] Atherosclerosis does not just develop in older adults. Autopsies of young soldiers who died during the Vietnam and Korean wars showed the presence of plaque in over 75 percent of their coronary arteries.[ii] One could argue that this may be due to the stress from war; however, similar results were obtained in more recent studies that examined the coronaries of young trauma victims.[iii] In a study published in the *Journal of the American Medical Association* in 1999, evidence of heart disease was seen in more than half of the fifteen- to nineteen-year-old group of the 2,876 study subjects.[iv] Thus, we should evaluate heart disease from a pediatric perspective and consider the habits of our children, since atherosclerosis can develop during childhood. Primary prevention of coronary artery disease should begin in adolescence with the right diet and lifestyle. It is no wonder that my son's pediatrician recommended that we switch him to skim milk at the age of two.

High cholesterol does not solely contribute to heart disease. Inflammation plays a large role as well. One does not need to have high cholesterol to have a heart attack. An emerging theory is one of endothelial dysfunction.[v] The endothelium lines the interior of our arteries much like a layer of carpet covers a floor. Any damage to the endothelium activates its repair system, which starts a cascade of events that begins with cholesterol squeezing through the damage and ends with plaque buildup that clogs the arteries. In order to stay healthy, the endothelium needs to produce nitric oxide, which is a gas released under stress that allows the vasculature to dilate. Increasing physical activity has been shown to improve endothelial function in patients with heart disease.[vi] High-fat foods, on the other hand, interfere with this important balance resulting in endothelial dysfunction.[vii] Diets focusing on low-fat, plant-based nutrition are an obvious recommendation to reduce heart disease, and the following section reviews the evidence supporting this conclusion.

Section 3 *Evidence for a Low-Fat, Vegan Diet to Reduce Heart Disease*

In order to understand the research described in this section, let's start with some definitions.

Vegetarian – a diet based on vegetables, beans, grains, and fruit that excludes meat and may include dairy and eggs.

Vegan or Plant-Based – a diet based on vegetables, beans, grains, and fruit excluding all animal products. In this book we use the terms vegan and plant-based interchangeably.

Shortly after my bypass, my sister-in-law recommended that I read *The China Study* by Dr. Colin Campbell.[viii] The book is based on an epidemiologic study done in the 1970s that evaluated the eating habits of the population of several counties in China. It correlated chronic illnesses and cancer in those regions to the people's diet. Although his conclusions were startling, they corresponded with previous epidemiologic studies regarding animal protein and chronic disease. By no means does this paragraph do justice to the whole book, but the following finding is significant: compared to economically poor Chinese, Dr. Campbell found that the more affluent segment of the population consumed more animal protein and incurred more chronic illnesses, such as heart disease and cancer. Americans, in general, consume large amounts of animal protein and fat, which, according to Campbell, puts us at risk for chronic disease. I had an opportunity to attend one of Dr. Campbell's lectures and was struck by his sincerity and dedication to convey his message on the benefits of plant-based foods.

I then reviewed the research conducted in the late 1980s by Dr. Dean Ornish. In a randomized, controlled trial, he demonstrated the reversal of heart disease in patients who were placed in his program, which included the following four components:

(1) An ultra-low-fat vegetarian diet, meaning 10 percent of total calories from fat, that included egg whites and skim milk but excluded oils, avocados, and nuts,

(2) A yoga program for stress management training,

(3) A group session for psychosocial support, and

(4) A moderate aerobic exercise program (such as walking).[ix]

Although the total number of patients in his study was small, it was elegantly done and statistically significant. Randomized, controlled trials are generally considered the gold standard in research. He also used state-of-the-art technology—cardiac angiograms—to show the reversal of heart disease. The more these patients adhered to his program, the more reversal they experienced in their cardiac diseases. Dr. Ornish has worked tirelessly to convey his message to others and even went on to write a *New York Times* Best Seller on reversing heart disease.[x] He was also featured on the covers of *Newsweek* and *Time* magazine.

The most amazing part about all of this is that the results of his low-tech intervention were far better than any advanced medical therapy available. Yet, in the last thirty years, his recommendation for a low-fat, vegetarian diet has not spread as much as blockbuster drugs. Why? Is it because our nation's system of medical reimbursement rewards providers for procedures and sick care rather than providing incentives to focus on wellness? Is it because there is so much confusion in the media regarding nutrition? Personally, I believe that physicians truly care about their patients and want to do the right thing, but nutrition has never been a strong focus in medical education. That is about to change.

Another study I reviewed was conducted in 1985 by Dr. Caldwell Esselstyn, a surgeon from the Cleveland Clinic. Dr. Esselstyn performed a longitudinal study in which he followed twenty-two patients with serious heart disease and placed them on a plant-based, low-fat diet.[xi] Like Dr. Ornish's diet, it consisted of less than 10 percent of calories from fat. Unlike the Ornish diet, Dr. Esselstyn did not permit eggs or dairy. Patients were also asked to moderate their consumption of alcohol and caffeine. He used diet and cholesterol lowering drugs to bring the total cholesterol of his patients below 150 mg/dL. He did not require his patients to do yoga or exercise. He monitored these patients and recorded cardiac events as they occurred. At the end of five years, eleven of eighteen patients were studied by angiography. The results revealed that 100 percent of them did not show progression of the disease, while 73 percent actually showed regression. He followed these patients for another seven years, and there were still no cardiac events in any of the patients who adhered to the diet.[xii] However, there were cardiac events in patients who reverted to their previous diet. Dr. Esselstyn's results further substantiate the results of Dr. Ornish's study.

He proved that a physician could influence a patient to adopt an ultra-low-fat diet that resulted in the halting or reversal of heart disease. He wrote a book called *Prevent and Reverse Heart Disease: The Revolutionary, Scientifically Proven, Nutrition-Based Care* and continues to actively write and lecture on that topic.[xiii] I agree with the observations he made in a recent lecture, that is, current medical therapy can, at best, only slow heart disease. It cannot stop it, as evidenced by the fact that patients return for more procedures.

When I had my heart attack, the American Heart Association (AHA) advocated a diet with less than 30 percent of calories from fat, a much more generous diet than those advocated by Drs. Ornish and Esselstyn. Since I never wanted to experience a heart attack again, I was willing to follow the more restrictive diets from the aforementioned researchers. It wasn't easy. Switching to a plant-based diet, excluding nuts and oils, were significant changes for me, but I was ready to do it.

It astonishes me that not all cardiologists and primary care physicians discuss this option with patients. Many argue that the Ornish and Esselstyn studies are too small; however, conducting a rigorous randomized controlled dietary study on a large scale is very difficult and not easily funded. These types of clinical trials require detailed accounting of eating habits, continuous compliance, and close researcher follow-up.

I believe there is enough evidence supporting a whole foods, plant-based, ultra-low-fat diet that it should be discussed as an option for all patients with heart disease. Thanks to support from my wife, we were able to adopt a low-fat, plant-based diet. The biggest challenge was finding simple, appetizing recipes, as we both lead busy lives managing our family and full time jobs.

To my amazement, I lost twenty-five pounds in only a few months after adopting the plant-based diet. A quick look at the literature revealed numerous studies that support my observation of weight loss after the adoption of this type of diet. A multicenter, randomized controlled trial on corporate employees showed that the adoption of a plant-based diet reduced body weight and lowered cardiovascular risk.[xiv] Scores of other studies show that vegetarians are slimmer than their meat-eating counterparts.[xv] When one considers other drastic measures such as bariatric surgery as a treatment for obesity, this may be a safer, more sustainable alternative.

Section 4 *Heart Disease: The Need for Change*

In the United States, $108.9 billion is spent annually on coronary heart disease and its sequela.[xvi] When the World Health Organization ranks countries in terms of health care costs per capita, the United States comes in first as being the most expensive. Countries such as France are lower on the list. If we rank countries by life expectancy, the United States ranks at thirty-five, on par with Cuba, while countries like Hong Kong and Japan are in the top five. There is no doubt in my mind that advanced technology and medical care do not account for this improved life expectancy; instead diet and lifestyle are the major contributing factors to increased longevity. As a nation we have the most expensive health care, but we do not have much to show for it.

According to a recent population study in the Journal of the American Medical Association, more than a third of Americans (36 percent) are obese.[xvii] As our lives get busier, fast food becomes an attractive option for many. According to the CDC, between 2007 and 2010, adults consumed an average of 11.3 percent of their daily calories from fast food.[xviii] Diets that are higher in fast food have higher calories and fewer nutrients.

The standard American diet (SAD) is high in animal proteins, fats, and processed foods. It provides insufficient fiber, complex carbohydrates, and nutrients.

On the other hand, a plant-based diet full of fat and refined grains will not prevent or reverse heart disease. If we eat hash browns, French fries, and white bread, we can claim to be vegetarians, but we cannot claim a healthy diet. It is important to focus on whole foods that are high in fiber and nutrients.

Section 5 *Other Dietary Considerations*

Protein

People often ask me, "How do you get enough protein on a plant-based diet?" In developed countries like the United States, people consume a great deal more protein that they actually need through meat-based diets. We simply eat far too much protein in the standard American diet. The Institutes of Medicine's Food and Nutrition Board publishes the Estimated Average Requirement (EAR) of proteins for adults in the United States, which is 0.6–0.7 grams per kilogram per day (gm/kg/day).[xix] This value is determined through nitrogen balance experiments, and the average adult weighing 150 pounds would need 40 grams of protein, or 160 calories from protein per day. The RDA or Recommended Daily Allowance of protein, on the other hand, is calculated by adding two standard deviations to the EAR and varies by age group.[xx] An adult man would need about 56 grams of protein based on the RDA. A whole-food, plant-based diet provides all the protein that we need. Let's review the following example of a healthy diet for one day, using some of the recipes from this book.

Breakfast:
Steel-cut oatmeal (1/2 cup dry) = 10 grams of protein
Blueberries (1/2 cup) = 0.5 gram of protein
Soymilk (1 cup) = 6 grams of protein

Snack:
Apple (1) = 0.3 gram of protein

Lunch:
Chilled Noodle Salad with Peaches (1 serving) = 25 grams of protein

Snack:
Celery and Hummus (6 tbsp.) = 6 grams of protein

Dinner:
Anytime Green Enchiladas (1 serving) = 13 grams of protein

Total protein: ~61 grams

In the past, people believed we had to eat plant foods in certain combinations within a meal to get all of the essential amino acids our bodies require, but new research indicates that is not the case. As long as we eat a variety of plant foods within a day, our protein needs can be easily met.[xxi] One should not need to take protein supplements.

Fiber

Fiber is sorely lacking in the average American diet, with most people consuming only half of what they need. The recommended daily allowance of fiber is 25–35 grams. Fiber absorbs water in the gut and provides bulk to stool, making it easier to pass. Consider the following clinically proven health benefits of fiber:

1. Preventing and alleviating hemorrhoids

2. Lowering the risk of heart disease

3. Lowering the risk of type 2 diabetes

4. Lowering the risk of diverticulitis and inflammatory diseases of the intestine

Fiber can be found in whole grains, fruits, and vegetables. When shopping for breads or cereals, read the nutrition label for the fiber content. A helpful label will break down the fiber by both soluble and insoluble. Soluble fiber has been associated with a decrease in cardio-vascular disease. Foods that are high in soluble fiber include oats (bran or oatmeal), beans, peas, brown rice, barley, citrus, and pears.

Manufacturers are adding marketing phrases to their packaging such as, "contains 5 grams of whole grains." This should not be equated with 5 grams of fiber. Check the label for the actual fiber content. While using whole grains is much more beneficial than using re-fined, enriched flour, many consumers mistakenly believe that they are increasing their fiber intake by the listed amount of whole grains.

Some products add extra fiber to their ingredients. Breads, English muffins, bagels, torti-llas, or pastas labeled as "carb-friendly" have higher fiber content, but you should still check the label. Breakfast is a great meal to get a good dose of your daily fiber requirements, as there are a large variety of foods from which you can choose.

There are several healthier substitutes for white rice, white pasta, and mashed potatoes. Consider the following substitutions.

Substitutions: Replacing Low Fiber Ingredients with Whole Grains

Instead of:	Grams of fiber per serving	Choose:	Grams of fiber per serving
White Rice	0.6	Quinoa	5.2
		Bulgur wheat	7.1
		Brown rice	3.5
White pasta	2.1	Whole-wheat pasta	3.9
		Brown rice pasta	3.9
Mashed potatoes	3.2	Roasted potatoes with skin	3.7

Another way to increase the amount of fiber in your diet is to replace meat dishes with vegetarian ones. Beans are an excellent source of fiber and protein. Unlike meat, they don't contain any cholesterol, are lower in fat, and are lower in calories, ounce for ounce. For example, one serving of steak is 4 ounces. A lean serving will contain 134 calories, 4 grams of fat, and no fiber. The same size serving of roasted, skinless chicken breast is 124 calories, 1.4 grams of fat, and no fiber. You can get roughly the same number of calories from 2/3 cups of cooked beans (e.g., kidney, navy, pinto, etc.). That's 140 calories, 1 gram of fat, 7.3 grams of fiber and 2 extra ounces of food. When watching caloric intake, eating a larger quantity of food also helps with satiety.

Ground flaxseed is a good source of fiber, and it is easy to add it to breakfast cereal. Flaxseed is also a source of omega-3 fatty acids. Dr. Esselstyn recommends taking one tablespoon of ground flaxseed a day to meet this requirement. Although the current data on flaxseed and heart disease may be insufficient to make a recommendation on the secondary prevention of coronary artery disease, the fiber content does help with satiety.

Sugar

There is far too much sugar in the standard American diet. It's insidious. Foods high in added sugar have extra calories with no added nutritional value. The average American consumes about 20 teaspoons of sugar a day.[xxii]

The American Heart Association recommends on average using no more than 9 teaspoons of added sugar a day for men and 6 teaspoons for women. Although we may not be adding sugar to our foods, it is present in processed foods, including ketchup, salad dressings, and pasta sauce. The World Health Organization (WHO) has recently announced that it is halving its recommendation for adults to 5 percent of total calories or about 6 teaspoons a day for an adult of normal weight.[xxiii]

A can of soda may contain 10 teaspoons or 40 grams of sugar. So, one could exceed the daily recommendations with just a can of soda. A study published in January 2014 concluded that too much added sugar could significantly increase ones risk of dying from cardiovascular disease—yet another reason to reduce sugar intake.[xxiv]

There are a few recipes in this book sweetened with a small amount of agave nectar. While it is an added sugar, it has a sweeter taste and a lower glycemic index than refined sugar. It should only be used in moderation and in accordance with the recommended guidelines.

Vitamin B-12

Vitamin B-12, which is manufactured by microbes, is found in animal foods. If you choose to switch completely to a plant-based diet, the recommendation is to take 1,000 micrograms (mcg) of B-12 a day. Taking 2,500 mcg a week would also suffice. It is important to work with your physician to measure B-12 levels periodically.

Section 6 *My Father: A Case in Point*

At this time, I should probably introduce you to my father. My parents immigrated to the United States from India in 1983. My father was forty-seven years old at that time. Two years later, at the age of forty-nine, he noticed heavy chest pain while at work in New York. He was about to write it off as indigestion. Fortunately, an astute coworker realized what was happening and called 911. He was rushed to the hospital where he was diagnosed with a heart attack. This was well before the time of coronary stenting. He was placed on bed rest for a month and scheduled for bypass surgery. As a high school sophomore, I remember visiting him at the hospital. His surgeon explained all the details of the surgery. Although I was terrified of the consequences, I marveled at the surgeon's ability, which guided me to a career in medicine. I felt powerless, and yet I wanted to help my father. I recall my father telling me that he had come across Dr. Ornish's revolutionary new approach, as his research article had just been published. Unfortunately at the time, the entire medical establishment did not hold this view, and he was soon encouraged to return to the standard American diet and reduce some of his fatty foods. After his surgery my father improved, but within a few years he developed crippling angina and had to give up working. His symptoms were controlled with medications.

Fourteen years later, I had completed medical school and a residency in internal medicine. I was working as a community physician in California. My father's anginal symptoms progressively worsened, and he experienced frequent chest pain and shortness of breath with walking only a few steps. He was living in Las Vegas, and his cardiologist determined that his bypass grafts were blocked. He attempted to put in a stent but was unable to do so. My father was subsequently seen by the cardiologists at the University of California, Davis. They were able to open up a blocked artery with a stent and his symptoms improved. A year later he developed chest pain and shortness of breath again, and his cardiologist found that he had developed disease within his stent so a smaller stent was deployed within the existing stent.

The next year he had similar symptoms, and again the cardiologist placed a stent within the previous stents. I was quite concerned and asked the cardiologist how long this could go on. I was told seven times. This could not continue, I thought. There had to be a way to break this cycle of forming plaque.

It was around this time that I had my heart attack and bypass surgery, which led to my adoption of a low-fat, plant-based diet absent of nuts and oil. I sat down with my parents and asked my father to consider switching to this diet and he readily agreed. My mother, who did all the cooking, worked hard to create American and traditional Indian meals with the dietary restrictions I laid out. He also engaged in a yoga and walking program. At first, it was hard for him to make the transition, but over time, he started to feel better and the positive results encouraged him to continue.

Within five months, I discovered that he was walking without shortness of breath or angina and spending more hours at the gym. His life was transformed from one of suffering with chest pain, frequent emergency room visits, and back and shoulder pain to a relatively pain free, enjoyable life. He started playing bocce ball and gardening. His attitude about life became much more positive. The change was so dramatic that I soon got a call from my mother asking me to do something because he was getting too active and driving her crazy. This was astonishing to all of us. I had no doubt in my mind that he had some reversal of his disease. This provided the motivation for both of us to continue on this plan. My father recently passed away, a few months after his eightieth birthday. He wanted others to know how this diet changed his life, and this provided me with some of the motivation to write this book. All of the recipes in this book are based on a low-fat, vegan diet, deriving 10 percent of its calories from fat. It excludes avocados, nuts, seeds, dairy, eggs, and added oils.

In the past five years, I have experienced no cardiac events and have had more energy than before my heart attack. I have participated in duathlons and have had the joy of coaching my boys' field hockey team.

Section 7 *Tips for Adopting a Low-Fat, Vegan Diet*

Having maintained a low-fat, plant-based diet for five years, I have come across a few pointers that make the switch to this lifestyle manageable. These tips focus on attitude, behaviors, and simple ways to modify traditional recipes.

Instead of dwelling on the foods this diet avoids, we can consider this a lifestyle of inclusion. Many of the foods included in this book are derived from recipes that span the globe and include a variety of flavors. Each meal is an adventure.

1. If you are currently eating the standard American diet, I suggest starting slowly. After all, Rome was not built in a day. Pick one day a week during which you will only eat plant-based foods. Over time, you can expand this to include more days.

2. Eat out less, and eat at home more. For this, it is essential that you learn how plant-based meals are prepared. The recipes in the next section will help you get started.

3. When eating out, I recommend calling the restaurant in advance to see if the chef can accommodate your diet. Most chefs will make accommodations if they are notified in advance.

4. Keep a list of restaurants that serve plant-based foods handy.

5. Shop at farmers markets. It will expose you to fresh and new vegetables.

6. Be willing to try a new dish and modify it if you need to.

7. Engage your family so that they do this with you. The support you give each other will make a big difference.

8. Feel free to experiment and convert your favorite recipes to a plant-based version. Cathi's tips in the next chapter will help with substitutes.

9. Celebrate the small steps you make. You are not only improving your health but you are also being kind to the environment.

Section 8 *Weight Loss*

As I mentioned earlier, switching from the standard American diet to a low-fat, vegan diet will likely result in weight loss for the vast majority of people. I lost twenty-five pounds within a few months of adopting this diet. If, after switching to this diet, you have not noticed any weight loss, and you want to lose weight, it may be necessary to count your calories.

The first step to weight loss is understanding how many calories your body needs based on your height, gender, and activity level. Rather than provide calculations in this book, I would refer you to one of the many calorie calculators available on the Internet. Your doctor or nutritionist can also help you determine this number. Consuming 500 calories per day less than what your body requires should result in losing one pound per week. Consuming 250 calories less per day should result in losing one pound in two weeks. Your desire for speedy weight loss or your tolerance for moderate hunger may determine how to best fit this with your lifestyle.

If you use a smart phone, there are several easy-to-use applications for tracking your calories on a daily basis. The advantage to this is the ready access of the phone. (No need to carry around a notebook or log onto your computer.) Many applications have calorie counts loaded for just about any food you might consume. Studies have shown that frequent, consistent self-monitoring of caloric intake is correlated to long-term success in weight management.[xxv]

Section 9 *Yoga*

Although this is a book focused on heart healthy recipes, I would be remiss if I ignored the value of exercise and stress reduction.

We are faced with a constant barrage of low-level stress, as we constantly check our smart phones, keep tabs on work, and meet the increasing demands of daily life in our culture. Constant, low-level stress may be more dangerous than intermittent stress because it is so insidious. Ironically, turning back to the ancient wisdom of yoga might provide a solution to this dilemma.

I lived in India until the age of thirteen. My parents were trained as yoga instructors, and although my mother instructed me in yoga when I was young, I paid no heed to it at the time. I intermittently attended yoga classes at the gym after I got married, but it was not until after my heart attack that I took a serious interest in it. I queried the scientific literature in 2014 and found 1,115 studies on the benefits of yoga. They range from studies on the treatment of mood and posttraumatic stress to muscular ailments such as back pain.

Dr. Herbert Benson, a cardiologist from Harvard, coined the term "relaxation response" to describe the body's ability to release chemicals that relax the muscles and increase blood flow to the brain. It is the opposite of the "fight or flight" response. In his book, *The Relaxation Response,* he demonstrated that the relaxation response can be used to counteract stress and can be activated by meditation.[xxvi]

There is a growing body of research that suggests that certain yoga techniques improve physical health by down-regulating the sympathetic nervous system—in other words, decreasing the body's "fight or flight" response system. The effects of yoga on stress management are well documented.[xxvii] Some studies also show that yoga decreases stress hormones such as cortisol and epinephrine when measured in the saliva and urine.[xxviii] There are further studies demonstrating that certain yoga exercises can lower blood pressure.[xxix,xxx]

Yoga combines exercise and meditation, which triggers the relaxation response. Calming the mind and reducing stress are among its benefits. A well-rounded yoga routine moves our bodies through a series of stretches and puts our joints through their full range of motion. As a yoga instructor, I teach two classes a month, and I have witnessed the positive effect on my students. By the end of each class, they have let go of their stress and are completely relaxed. Some of them actually fall asleep during the *savasana* or relaxation phase at the end.

Always check with your doctor before starting a yoga routine and do not use it as a substitute for medical care. Please consider the following safety tips:

1. Keep a slight bend in your knees to protect your back.

2. Come out of a pose if it causes pain or feels uncomfortable. The old adage "no pain, no gain" does not apply here.

3. Understand that yoga is not a competitive sport. We all have different levels of flexibility, and we may find ourselves with different levels of flexibility on different days.

4. Find a studio or gym with an instructor who will listen to you and demonstrate modifications for poses.

5. Inform instructors of any injury you have so they can adjust the routine to prevent further injury.

Section 10 *Exercise*

As a nation, we are quite sedentary. In fact the average American takes only 5,500 steps per day. This is far short of other countries such as France and China.[xxxi] There has also been increasing evidence that sitting for too long may be harmful.[xxxii] This has led some to compare sitting to smoking as a risk factor for heart disease. The benefits of exercise on the other hand are too numerous to quantify. If one could bottle its benefits in a pill, everyone would buy it, and it would become a blockbuster.

What can we do to change our trajectory if we are sedentary? We certainly don't need fancy equipment or a special gym. A simple activity, such as walking, will suffice. I generally recommend walking thirty to forty-five minutes most days of the week, and if you do more, that is even better. Exercising with family or friends makes it more enjoyable. For those who are able, jogging, bicycling, or engaging in aerobic classes such as Zumba and boot camp are other options. Even an activity such as gardening provides us with exercise. Adding strength training provides further benefits. It is far more important to have a regular exercise program than to embark on sporadic bursts of strenuous exercise. As always, please check with your physician before beginning a new exercise routine.

Tips from Cathi's Kitchen

Planet-friendly Benefits of a Vegetarian Diet

Ever wonder how much fresh water is used to grow the food we eat? According to a summary by York,[xxxiii] industrial agriculture consumes approximately 75 percent of the freshwater used globally. Meat production uses up to one hundred times more water than growing vegetables. According to Gleick,[xxxix] it takes roughly 500 to 1500 liters of water to grow 1 kilogram of potatoes, but it takes 15,000 to 70,000 liters of water to raise 1 kilogram of beef.

York also cites studies that attribute the following environmental impacts to livestock production:

9 percent of carbon dioxide emissions (not counting respiration)

37 percent of methane emissions

65 percent of nitrous oxide emissions

Introduction

I did not grow up in a vegetarian or vegan household, so switching our family to a vegan diet was daunting at first, but the more I learned, the more inspired I became. Before Rajiv's heart attack, we had already started "going green." We had planted a garden, started shopping at the farmer's market, and began composting our kitchen scraps. We even put solar panels on our house, knowing that someday we'd get an electric car. Plant-based diets are ecofriendly. I consider it an extra bonus. Doing something that is good for our bodies is also good for our planet. Throughout the book, I included several "green" tips and facts that have inspired me.

I hope the kitchen tips in this chapter will facilitate your transition to this diet. I have included tips on shopping for groceries, planning meals, preparing foods from bulk, and cooking food without oil.

Section 1 *Grocery Shopping: Menus and Shopping Lists*

Planning meals in advance and creating a shopping list takes a little time, but organization makes cooking much easier. Leftovers for lunch also decrease the amount of time spent in the kitchen. When shopping, look for whole, less refined, foods. For example, choose brown rice instead of white rice. Here are a couple of sample weekly menu plans and shopping lists to help you get started.

Spring–Summer Menu Planner

Days	Breakfast	Lunch	Dinner
Sunday	Apricot and Peach Breakfast Cobbler	Bean Salad with Summer Vegetables	Indian Beet Burgers with Roasted Potatoes
Monday	Steel-Cut Oatmeal with Blueberries	Leftover Indian Beet Burgers with Roasted Potatoes	Summer Vegetables over Pasta (Ratatouille)
Tuesday	Leftover Apricot and Peach Breakfast Cobbler	Leftover Bean Salad with Summer Vegetables	Leeks, Mushrooms, and Kidney Beans in a White Wine Sauce
Wednesday	Cold High-Fiber Cereal with Almond Milk and Bananas	Leftover Summer Vegetables over Pasta (Ratatouille)	Sambar Potato Bajji
Thursday	Steel-Cut Oatmeal with Blueberries	Leftover Leeks, Mushrooms, and Kidney Beans in a White Wine Sauce	Fruit and Pepper Medley
Friday	Cold High-fiber Cereal with Almond Milk and Bananas	Leftover Fruit and Pepper Medley	Tacos de Verano
Saturday	Scrambled Tofu and Whole-wheat Toast	Leftover Sambar Potato Bajji	Sushi Salad

Spring–Summer Shopping List (Copy list and double-check pantry and refrigerator to scratch off items already on hand)

Whole-wheat flour (5-lb. bag)
Nutritional yeast (1/4 c.)
Egg replacer (check health food aisle)
Baking powder
Agave nectar
Corn starch
Sambar masala
Cinnamon
Curry powder
Salt
Pepper, black
Cumin, seeds
Cumin, ground
Ginger paste
Italian seasoning
Turmeric
Coriander, ground
Cayenne pepper
Applesauce (unsweetened)
Soymilk (1 qt.)
Almond milk (2 qts.)
Peaches (5)
Apricots (13)
Nectarines (2)
Tofu, firm, low-fat (2 pkgs.)
Onion, yellow (6½)
Bell pepper, green (1½)
Lettuce, red leaf, (1 bunch)
Green chilies, diced (4-oz. can)
Onion, red (1)
Bell pepper, red (3)
Bell pepper, yellow (1)

Corn, sweet (4 cobs)
Cherry tomatoes (1 pkg.)
Cucumber (3)
Salad greens (6 oz.)
Potatoes, medium russet (6)
Potatoes, small red (2 lbs.)
Beets (3)
Carrots (3)
Eggplant (1)
Zucchini (5)
Squash, yellow (2)
Tomatoes (7)
Spinach, fresh (6 oz.)
Basil (1 bunch)
Garlic (2 bulbs)
Cilantro (2 bunches)
Leeks (2)
Mushrooms (10 oz.)
Celery (1 bunch)
Rotini pasta, whole-wheat (14-oz. pkg.)
Brown rice (5-lb. bag)
Tomato paste (1 6-oz. can)
Tomatoes, canned (Italian style, 15 oz.)
Black beans (2 cans)
Black-eyed peas (1 can)
Lime juice
Lemon juice (1/4 c)
Corn tortillas (1 pkg. of 10)
Nori (dried seaweed sushi wrappers, 1 pkg.)
Pickled daikon
Edamame, frozen (1 pkg.)

Continued from page 26

Raisins

Oatmeal, steel-cut (3–4 cups)

Cereal, high fiber

White wine (1 bottle)

Rice vinegar

Red wine vinegar

Apple cider vinegar

Fall–Winter Menu Planner

Days	Breakfast	Lunch	Dinner
Sunday	Butternut Squash Waffles	Ginger Tofu and Julienned Vegetables with Noodles	Winter-Red Enchilada Casserole
Monday	Steel-Cut Oatmeal with Blueberries	Leftover Winter-Red Enchilada Casserole	Cannellini Bean and Bulgur Wheat Burgers
Tuesday	Leftover Butternut Squash waffles	Leftover Ginger Tofu and Julienned Vegetables with Noodles	Mushroom Stroganoff
Wednesday	Cold High-Fiber Cereal with Almond Milk and Bananas	Leftover Cannellini Bean and Bulgur Wheat Burgers	Curried Vegetable Wrap
Thursday	Steel-Cut Oatmeal with Blueberries	Leftover Curried Vegetable Wrap	Calzones with Spinach and Tofu
Friday	Cranberry Orange Bread	Leftover Calzones with Spinach and Tofu	Pasta Verde
Saturday	French Toast Casserole	Leftover Pasta Verde	Stuffed Sweet Dumpling Squash

Winter–Fall Shopping List (Copy list and double-check pantry and refrigerator to scratch off items already on hand)

Whole-wheat flour (5-lb. bag)
Pepper, black
Salt
Baking soda
Baking powder
Cornstarch
Egg replacer
Applesauce
Rosemary
Vanilla
Cinnamon
Curry powder
Flax seed
Agave nectar
Soy sauce
Nutritional yeast (¼ cup)
Orange juice
Apple juice
Lemon juice
Almond milk, unsweetened (2 qts.)
Soymilk, nonfat (1 qt.)
Potatoes, medium russet (6)
Potatoes, red (1 lb.)
Broccoli (3 heads)
Carrots (10)
Onion, yellow (5)
Sweet dumpling squash (4)
Brown rice (1 pkg.)
Lettuce, romaine (1 head)
Basil leaves (1 bunch)
Mushrooms (16 oz.)
Celery roots (2)
Broccoli (1 head)

Butternut squash
Cranberries, fresh (1 pkg.)
Tofu, extra firm (3 pkgs.)
Ginger, fresh
Garlic (3 bulbs)
Cauliflower (1 head)
Tomatoes (4)
Cabbage, red (1 head)
Mango chutney (1 jar)
Cannellini beans (2 cans)
Kidney beans (1 can)
Bulgur wheat (1 cup)
Whole-wheat bread (1 loaf)
Whole-wheat hamburger buns
Whole-wheat bread dough, frozen (1 loaf)
Spinach, frozen (16-oz. pkg.)
Peas, frozen (1 pkg.)
Whole-wheat bread (1 loaf)
Blueberries, frozen (2 pkgs.)
Pizza sauce (nonfat)
Red enchilada sauce (28 oz.)
Vegetable stock (1 qt.)
Oatmeal, steel-cut (3–4 cups)
Cereal, high fiber
White wine (1 bottle)
Worcestershire sauce
Whole-wheat eggless noodles (1 pkg.)
Whole-wheat linguine (14 oz.) (or soba noodles, 14 oz.)
Whole-wheat pasta, rotini (16-oz. pkg.)
Tortillas, whole-wheat, soft taco size
Tortillas, whole-wheat, burrito size, (1 pkg. of 8)

Section 2 *Reading Nutrition Labels*

Reading nutrition labels provides us with important, basic information about the food we purchase. The government has a website that provides detailed instructions on how to read the information contained in nutrition labels: http://www.fda.gov/food/ ingredientspackaginglabeling/labelingnutrition/ucm274593.htm. I recommend focusing on these two key aspects of the nutrition label:

1. Total fat. With very few exceptions, purchase foods with zero grams of fat. Tofu and almond milk have a small amount of fat, which this book includes in moderation.

2. Added fat. If a product has added oil, but the total quantity is less than 0.5 gram per serving, the nutrition label will round the quantity of fat down to zero. To avoid added oil, it is necessary to read the ingredients to ensure no extra fat is included.

Section 3 *Preparing Food From Bulk*

Many of the recipes in this book will call for prepared beans or grains. The following is a quick reference on how to prepare foods from their dried forms. The recipes in this book can be made with canned beans or dried beans that have already been prepared.

Dried beans

One pound of dried beans will yield approximately 7–8 cups of cooked beans. The quick method of preparing dried beans is as follows. First, wash the beans in a strainer. Then add 10 cups of water to a large pot, add beans, and bring to a boil. Once boiling, turn the heat down to medium simmer and cover. Cook the beans for one and a half hours, or until beans are tender. We have also found that cooking beans with an electric pressure cooker can save time. Consider cooking one pound at a time and freezing the beans in 2-cup quantities for easy use.

Bulgur wheat, whole-wheat couscous, and quinoa

As mentioned elsewhere in this book, bulgur wheat and quinoa are great substitutes for rice due to their higher fiber content. For busy cooks, it is also nice that they cook so quickly in comparison with white or brown rice. For each cup of bulgur wheat, whole-wheat cous-cous, or quinoa, boil 2 cups of water or vegetable stock. Once boiling, add the grain or pasta, cover, and turn heat down to simmer for 10–15 minutes, or until all of the water has been absorbed.

Brown rice

Brown rice requires the same ratio of grain to water as bulgur wheat and quinoa (i.e., 1 to 2). The only difference is the time required to cook it. First, wash the brown rice in a strainer. Boil the desired quantity of water in a large pot, add the rice, and turn the heat down to sim-mer. Cover and cook for 45–50 minutes, or until water is absorbed. Alternatively, place the rice and water in a rice cooker, and follow the directions that came with the appliance. Since brown rice has a long cook-time, it is handy to keep packets of cooked rice in the freezer so it is ready for a quick thaw in the microwave. Similar to dried beans, consider freezing in 2-cup quantities.

Steel-cut oatmeal

Steel-cut oatmeal takes a long time to prepare, especially compared to instant oatmeal, but the time is worth it in terms of taste, nutritional quality, and fiber content. Consider cooking a large batch and storing the leftovers in the refrigerator for a quick and easy break-fast later in the week. To cook the steel-cut oatmeal, boil 3½ cups of water for every 1 cup of cereal. Once boiling, turn heat down to simmer for 30–40 minutes or until the water is fully absorbed. Stir twice while simmering.

Section 4 *Cooking Without Fat and Preparing Meatless Meals*

Traditionally, sautéing food generally requires oil in the pan, which is helpful to prevent food from sticking to the pan. Since the recipes in the book completely omit oil, using a non-stick pan on the stove is very helpful. As vegetables brown, adding a splash of water, wine, lemon juice, or vegetable broth can prevent sticking.

Clean-up after baking is easiest if pans are lined with parchment paper. Nonstick bake-ware is also helpful. Many baked goods call for butter, oil, or shortening. In this book, we often use applesauce as a substitute.

Many of the recipes in this book originally contained meat, but substituting eggplant, beans, seitan, mushrooms, or tofu turned old-time favorites into healthier alternatives. Replacing cow's milk with unsweetened almond milk or low-fat soymilk was also a fairly simple switch.

Below is a list of kitchenware, tools, and appliances that may be helpful in preparing some of the meals in this book.

Nonstick pans
High-horsepower blender
Immersion blender
Food processor
Rice cooker (optional)
Electric pressure cooker (optional)
Waffle iron
Griddle
Bread machine
Parchment paper

Breakfast ideas

Planet-friendly Benefits of a Vegetarian Diet

According to Pimentel in an article published in the American Society for Clinical Nutrition, it takes significantly less energy to produce grain-based protein than animal-based protein. Generating 1 kcal of grain-based protein requires 2.2 kcal of fossil energy. Energy required to generate animal-based protein varies by the type of animal raised. On average, it requires 25 kcal of fossil energy to produce 1 kcal of animal protein. Fossil fuels are used for fertilizers, agricultural machinery, fuel, irrigation, and pesticides. Considering fossil fuels are a finite resource, organic, vegetarian diets are the most sustainable.[xxxv]

Apricot and Peach Breakfast Cobbler

2 c. whole-wheat flour
1 tbsp. baking powder
1 tsp. cinnamon
½ c. applesauce
2 tbsp. agave nectar
2 tbsp. powdered egg replacer
½ c. water
½ c. nonfat soymilk
5 peaches, diced
10 apricots, diced

In a large bowl, mix flour, baking powder, and cinnamon. In a small bowl, combine egg replacer and water. In a third bowl, combine applesauce, agave nectar, egg replacement mixture, and soymilk. Then, add the wet ingredients to the dry and mix thoroughly with a wooden spoon. Line a 9x13-inch baking pan with parchment paper. Cover the paper with the fruit, then evenly dollop with dough mixture. Bake at 400°F and bake for 20–25 minutes or until a knife inserted into the dough comes out clean.

Serves 8

EACH SERVING CONTAINS:
186 calories, 1 gram of fat, 6 grams of fiber.

Buckwheat Blueberry Pancakes

1 c. buckwheat flour
1 c. whole-wheat flour
1 tsp. baking soda
1 tsp. baking powder
½ tsp. salt
2 tbsp. powdered egg replacer
¼ c. applesauce
2 c. water
1½ c. blueberries

Mix dry ingredients in a large mixing bowl. Add egg replacer, applesauce, and water and mix with a wooden spoon until well blended. Fold in blueberries. (If using frozen blueberries, thaw and rinse first.) Heat nonstick griddle to 350°F. To ensure griddle is hot enough, splash a small amount of water on it. If it sizzles immediately, the griddle is ready. Spoon mix onto griddle, forming pancakes approximately 4 inches in diameter, and cook for approximately 4–5 minutes or until several bubbles have formed on top of each pancake. Flip pancakes and cook for another 3–4 minutes, or until the centers are fully cooked.

Serves 4

EACH SERVING CONTAINS:
280 calories, 1 gram of fat, 7 grams of fiber.

Butternut Squash Waffles

½ medium butternut squash
1½ c. whole-wheat flour
½ c. milled flax seed
1 tsp. baking soda
1 tsp. baking powder
½ tsp. salt
3 tbsp. powdered egg replacer
¾ c. water
¼ c. applesauce
1½ c. nonfat soymilk

In advance, wash butternut squash, slice lengthwise, scoop out seeds, and bake at 350°F for 50–60 minutes, until softened. Scoop out squash (i.e., remove from outer skin) and mash it. In a large bowl, combine dry ingredients. Then, mix in egg replacer, water, applesauce, soymilk, and squash. Follow directions of waffle iron to cook.

Serves 4

EACH SERVING CONTAINS:
311 calories, 5 grams of fat, 13 grams of fiber.

Cranberry Orange Bread

2 c. whole-wheat flour
1½ tsp. baking powder
½ tsp. baking soda
¾ tsp. salt
½ c. agave nectar
¾ c. orange juice
¼ c. applesauce
2 tbsp. powdered egg replacer
½ c. water
1 c. cranberries

Mix dry ingredients in large bowl. Add agave nectar, orange juice, applesauce, egg replacer, and water. Mix in thoroughly with a wooden spoon. Fold in cranberries. Pour into loaf pan and bake at 350°F for 50–60 minutes or until knife inserted comes out clean.

Serves 8

EACH SERVING CONTAINS:
194 calories, 0.5 gram of fat, 4.5 grams of fiber.

Eggplant "Sausage" Open-faced Breakfast Sandwiches

1 large globe eggplant, sliced ½ inch thick
2 tsp. sage
1 tsp. salt
1 tsp. black pepper
¼ tsp. tarragon
1 tbsp. brown sugar
¼ tsp. red pepper
¼ tsp. cloves
½ tsp. nutmeg
2 tbsp. whole-wheat flour
2 tomatoes, sliced ½ inch thick
1 pkg. firm tofu, light
4 whole-wheat English muffins
Salt to taste

Line one or two baking sheets with parchment paper. (The number of baking sheets will depend on the size of the eggplant.) Place eggplant slices on baking sheet and sprinkle with salt. Let the eggplant sweat for 30 minutes. In a gallon-sized plastic storage bag, combine sage, 1 tsp. salt, black pepper, tarragon, brown sugar, red pepper, cloves, nutmeg and flour. After the eggplant has sweated for 30 minutes, place one slice in the plastic bag and coat with flour and spices. Place back on baking sheet and repeat for remaining slices of eggplant. Slice tofu into four pieces along the long edge, resulting in ¼ inch thick rectangles, and place on baking sheet with eggplant. Bake at 350°F for 20 minutes. Place slices of tomato on a separate baking sheet and broil for 4–5 minutes. Toast English muffins. To assemble sandwiches, lay each half of the English muffin face-up on a plate. Add a slice of eggplant, tomato, and top with the tofu.

Serves 4

EACH SERVING CONTAINS:
234 calories, 4 grams of fat, 8 grams of fiber.

French Toast Casserole

10 slices whole-wheat bread, torn into bite-sized pieces
4 tbsp. powdered egg replacer
1 c. water
2¼ c. nonfat soy milk
3 tbsp. agave nectar
1 tsp. vanilla
1 tsp. cinnamon
1½ c. blueberries (or other diced seasonal fruit)

Place bread cubes in a 9x13 inch pan. Mix egg replacer, water, agave nectar, and vanilla, and pour into pan over bread, soaking all of the pieces. Top with blueberries and sprinkle with cinnamon. Bake at 350°F for 45–50 minutes.

Serves 6

EACH SERVING CONTAINS:
239 calories, 2 grams of fat, 11 grams of fiber.

Healthy Heart Apple Cake

3 c. whole-wheat flour
1½ tsp. baking powder
1½ tsp. baking soda
1 tsp. cinnamon
12 oz. apple juice concentrate (thawed if frozen)
1 c. applesauce, unsweetened
2 tbsp. powdered egg replacer
½ c. water
1 tsp. vanilla
4 apples, chopped (not peeled)

Line a 9x13 inch baking dish with parchment paper. Mix dry ingredients (flour, baking soda, baking powder, and cinnamon) in a bowl. In a separate bowl, mix concentrated juice, applesauce, egg replacer, water, and vanilla. Then add wet ingredients to the dry ingredients and combine thoroughly with a wooden spoon. Fold in apples. Pour into pan (batter will be thick), and bake at 350°F for 35 minutes.

Serves 12

EACH SERVING CONTAINS:
217 calories, 0.5 gram of fat, 5 grams of fiber.

Healthy Heart Muffins

¾ c. whole-wheat flour
¾ c. oat bran
½ c. milled flax seeds
2 tsp. baking powder
2 tsp. baking soda
½ tsp. salt
½ tsp. cinnamon
½ c. concentrated apple juice (thawed if frozen)
¼ c. agave nectar
½ c. applesauce
½ c. pumpkin puree
2 tbsp. powdered egg replacer
½ c. water
½ c. nonfat soymilk
½ c. raisins

In one bowl, combine whole-wheat flour, oat bran, flax seeds, baking powder, baking soda, salt, and cinnamon. In another bowl, combine the concentrated apple juice, agave nectar, applesauce, pumpkin, egg replacer, water, and soymilk. Pour wet mixture into dry and mix thoroughly. Fold in raisins. Spoon into muffin pan and bake at 350°F for 15 minutes or until a knife inserted comes out clean.

Variations: this recipe is very versatile. While keeping the dry ingredients constant, you can vary the pureed vegetable. Here are some options: carrots, zucchini, yellow squash, butternut squash. You can substitute the raisins with fresh blueberries, dried fruit, or chopped apple.

Makes 15 muffins

EACH SERVING CONTAINS:
106 calories, 2 grams of fat, 3 grams of fiber.

Oatmeal Raisin Breakfast Scones

1 c. whole-wheat flour
3 tbsp. agave nectar
1½ tsp. baking powder
½ tsp. ground cinnamon
1/3 c. applesauce
1 c. quick-cooking rolled oats
1 tbsp. powdered egg replacer
¼ c. water
¼ c. nonfat soymilk
¾ c. raisins

Line a baking sheet with parchment paper. Mix dry ingredients in a large bowl. Add egg substitute and soymilk. Fold in raisins. Spoon onto baking sheet. Bake at 400°F for 10–12 minutes.

Makes 8 scones

EACH SERVING CONTAINS:
166 calories, 1 gram of fat, 4 grams of fiber.

Chickpea Omelets

¾ c. garbanzo bean flour (also called chickpea or besan flour)
¾ c. water
½ onion, finely diced
4 oz. diced green chilies
½ tsp. salt

With a wire whisk, mix garbanzo bean flour, water, and salt until all lumps are gone. (Another option is to put the ingredients into a blender to combine until smooth.) Fold in onion and chilies. Set burner to medium heat, and place nonstick skillet on it for a few minutes to heat up. Once hot, pour mixture into pan. Cook for 4–5 minutes, watching closely to make sure mixture doesn't burn. With a spatula, cut mixture into quarters and flip-over to finish cooking, usually another 3–4 minutes.

Serves 4

EACH SERVING CONTAINS:
91 calories, 1 gram of fat, 2 grams of fiber.

Scrambled Tofu

½ onion, diced
½ green bell pepper, diced
1 pkg. tofu
½ tsp. curry powder
Salt and pepper to taste

Using a nonstick skillet, brown onion and green pepper. Crumble in tofu and mix in curry powder, salt, and pepper. Heat thoroughly, roughly 3–4 minutes on medium-high heat.

Serves 2

EACH SERVING CONTAINS:
158 calories, 6 grams of fat, 3 grams of fiber.

Breakfast Burritos

3 c. cannellini beans
1 onion, diced
1 tsp. sage
1 tsp. oregano
1 tsp. thyme
6 oz. fresh spinach
2 yellow squash, diced
Whole-wheat tortillas, burrito size
Salt and pepper to taste.

Using a dry, nonstick skillet, sauté onion and squash. If vegetables cook too quickly or start to burn, turn down heat and splash 1–2 tbsp. of water in the pan. Add herbs and cannellini beans. Once everything has heated through (roughly 3–4 minutes), add spinach and cook until lightly wilted. Add salt and pepper to taste. Remove from heat. Separate mixture into eight equal quantities. Spoon one quantity into the center of a tortilla. To make the wraps, fold the edge of the tortilla that's closest to you over the mixture, then fold the sides toward the center, and then roll the burrito away from you. Serve with salsa if desired.

Serves 8

EACH SERVING CONTAINS:
151 calories, 1 gram of fat, 15 grams of fiber.

High Protein Hot Cereal

1 c. lentils
1 c. steel-cut oatmeal
5 c. water
1 c. almond milk
1 yam, peeled and diced
1 cinnamon stick
1 tsp. nutmeg

In a large pot, combine oatmeal, yam, 2 c. water, almond milk, cinnamon stick, and nutmeg. Bring to a boil, then turn down heat and simmer for 30 minutes. In a separate pot, boil 3 c. water and 1 c. lentils, then simmer for 20–30 minutes. Drain lentils, then combine with oatmeal and serve.

Serves 8

EACH SERVING CONTAINS:
187 calories, 2 grams of fat, 10 grams of fiber.

RhubAppleCherry Pancake Topper

3 stalks rhubarb, sliced crosswise in ½ inch pieces
2 c. apples, diced in ½ inch chunks
1 14.5 oz. can cherries in water
1/3 c. agave nectar
¼ tsp. nutmeg
¼ tsp. cardamom powder
½ tsp. cinnamon
2 tsp. balsamic vinegar
1 tsp. cornstarch

Drain water from cherries into a bowl. In a skillet, braise rhubarb and apples in water from can of cherries for approximately 5 minutes or until tender. Add cherries, spices, vinegar and cornstarch. Set to medium heat, stir frequently to prevent burning, and cook until sauce thickens.

Serves 4

EACH SERVING CONTAINS:
173 calories, 0 grams of fat, 4 grams of fiber.

Green Power Smoothie

½ banana, frozen
1 apple, diced
2 kale leaves, stems removed
½ c. soybeans, frozen
¾ c. apple juice
1 tsp. ginger, grated
½ c. water

Place all ingredients into a very high-powered blender. Start at a slow speed and increase speed as ingredients become incorporated. Blend approximately one minute or until smooth.

Serves 2

EACH SERVING CONTAINS:
247 calories, 6 grams of fat, 4 grams of fiber.

Black Forest Smoothie

3 dates, pitted
12 cherries, frozen, pitted
¼ c. blueberries, frozen
½ orange, seeded, peeled
1 handful spinach, fresh
8 baby carrots (or 1 large carrot, peeled and cut into chunks)
¼ c. soybeans, frozen (edamame)
¼ tsp. amla powder (optional)
1 tbsp. flax seed, milled
¼ tsp. cinnamon
1 tbsp. cocoa powder
1 c. hibiscus tea (prepared using 1 c. water and 1 teabag)

Place all ingredients into a very high-powered blender. Start at a slow speed and increase speed as ingredients become incorporated. Blend approximately one minute or until smooth.

Serves 2

EACH SERVING CONTAINS:
266 calories, 4 grams of fat, 10 grams of fiber.

Orange Antioxidant Blast Smoothie

1 nectarine, pit removed, quartered and frozen
1 c. papaya, frozen
½ c. mango, frozen
½ orange, seeded and peeled
8 baby carrots (or 1 large carrot, peeled and cut into chunks)
1 c. soymilk
2 tbsp. flax seeds, milled
½ tsp. amla powder (optional)

Place all ingredients into a very high-powered blender. Start at a slow speed and increase speed as ingredients become incorporated. Blend approximately 1 minute or until smooth.

Serves 2

EACH SERVING CONTAINS:
146 calories, 1 gram of fat, 6 grams of fiber.

Salads

Five Simple Tips to Reducing Kitchen Waste

As we've mentioned earlier, vegetarian diets are more sustainable, but we can do even more to help the environment when we cook. This section focuses on what we can do to reduce the waste that ends up in landfills.

1. Compost vegetable scraps. Keeping compost bins in our yards to break down discarded vegetable scraps is a great way to put that organic matter to good use. Once the compost is ready, we can add it to our landscaping, providing extra nutrients for our plants.

2. Bring reusable grocery bags to the store. We can prevent waste in the first place by reusing grocery sacks.

3. Replace paper towels with cloth towels. Even if the paper towels are made from recycled materials, the paper came from trees at some point. Washing and drying towels does take energy, but we can minimize this by line-drying the towels.

4. Buy in bulk to reduce packaging waste. Prepackaged foods are generally more expensive than their bulk counterparts, and a lot of material goes into the packaging. We can minimize waste by buying bulk products and storing them in reusable containers.

5. Recycle as much as possible. Recycling does take energy, and a lot of what we toss into the recycling bin gets shipped overseas,[xxxvi] using even more energy, but at least the materials are not completely going to waste in a landfill.

Bean Salad with Summer Vegetables

¼ c. rice vinegar
¼ c. red wine vinegar
2 tbsp. raisins
3 cloves garlic
½ bunch cilantro
4 oz. diced green chilies
1 red onion, diced
1 red bell pepper, diced
1½ c. black beans
1½ c. black-eyed peas
2 cobs corn, kernels removed
1 c. cherry tomatoes, halved
1 cucumber, diced
6 oz. mixed salad greens
Salt to taste

In a blender or food processor, combine vinegars, raisins, garlic, cilantro, and chilies to make dressing. In a large bowl, combine onion, red bell pepper, black beans, black-eyed peas, corn kernels, cherry tomatoes, and cucumber. Toss with dressing. Serve over salad greens.

Serves 4

EACH SERVING CONTAINS:
273 calories, 2 grams of fat, 13 grams of fiber.

Carrot and Raisin Salad

5 c. of carrots, shredded
1½ c. of celery, chopped
1 c. silken tofu
¼ c. lemon juice
¾ c. of raisins
2 tsp. of agave nectar
1 tsp. of mustard
¼ tsp. of salt

In a blender, combine tofu, mustard, agave nectar, salt, and lemon juice. In a bowl, combine the carrots, celery, raisins, and dressing.

Serves 10

EACH SERVING CONTAINS:
75 calories, 1 gram of fat, 3 grams of fiber.

Chilled Noodle Salad with Peaches

½ bunch basil
½ bunch mint
½ bunch cilantro
1/3 c. agave nectar
1/3 c. lemon juice
1/3 c. water
1 jalapeño, seeded (optional)
4 cloves garlic
2 carrots, peeled and sliced thinly
2 cucumbers, sliced thinly
4 green onions, sliced thinly
3 c. sunflower sprouts (or substitute 2 c. bean sprouts)
2 peaches, diced
8 oz. Seitan
1 pkg. soba noodles
Low sodium soy sauce to taste

Prepare soba noodles according to package directions. Drain in colander and rinse with cold water. In a food processor with the mixing blade, combine basil, mint, cilantro, agave nectar, lemon juice, water, jalapeño, and garlic to make the dressing. Set aside. Rinse the food processor and reassemble with the slicing blade. Use the food processor to slice carrots, cucumbers, and onions. In a large pasta bowl, toss noodles, dressing, vegetables, and peaches.

Serves 5

EACH SERVING CONTAINS:
382 calories, 2 grams of fat, 6 grams of fiber.

Cucumber and Tomato Salad

1 cucumber, peeled and diced
2 large tomatoes, diced (heirloom tomatoes work nicely but aren't necessary)
4 tbsp. red wine vinegar
4 tbsp. fresh mint, chopped
Salt to taste

Mix all ingredients in a bowl and chill for 30 minutes.

Serves 4

EACH SERVING CONTAINS:
30 calories, 0 grams of fat, 1 gram of fiber.

Curried Rice and Artichoke Salad

4 c. brown rice, cooked
1 red bell pepper, diced
4 green onions, chopped
15 oz. garbanzo beans
13.75 oz. artichoke hearts, quartered
3 tbsp. red wine vinegar
2 tsp. garlic paste
1½ tsp. curry powder
½ c. silken tofu
2 tbsp. lemon juice
Salt to taste

In a blender, combine vinegar, garlic paste, curry powder, tofu, and lemon juice. In a large bowl, toss brown rice, bell pepper, onions, garbanzo beans, and artichoke hearts. Pour dressing over salad and mix together. Salt to taste.

Serves 4

EACH SERVING CONTAINS:
335 calories, 4 grams of fat, 9 grams of fiber.

Gazpacho Salad

4 tomatoes, diced
2 cucumbers, peeled, seeded, and diced
2 red bell peppers, diced
8 oz. super firm tofu, drained and cubed
Salt to taste
1 bunch romaine lettuce, washed and torn into bite-sized pieces

Dressing
½ c. silken tofu
¼ c. lime juice
2 scallions
1 tsp. red wine vinegar
2 cloves garlic
¼ tsp. cayenne pepper

Place firm tofu cubes onto cookie sheet lined with parchment paper and bake at 400°F for 30 minutes. Divide lettuce onto four plates. In a mixing bowl, combine tomatoes, cucumbers, bell peppers, and baked tofu. In a blender, combine all of the ingredients for the salad dressing. Place vegetables and baked tofu in a bowl and toss with dressing. Distribute evenly over lettuce.

Serves 4

EACH SERVING CONTAINS:
175 calories, 4 grams of fat, 3 grams of fiber.

Hot (or Cold) Pasta Salad

Dressing
¼ c. balsamic vinegar
½ c. red wine vinegar
2 cloves garlic, chopped
½ tsp. salt
¼ tsp. black pepper, crushed
2 tsp. basil, dried
2 tsp. oregano, dried

Pasta salad
1 14 oz. pkg. whole-wheat rotini or penne pasta
1 16 oz. jar marinated three-bean salad (no oil added)
1 bunch broccoli florets, chopped
1 head cauliflower, chopped
1 can artichoke hearts, drained and quartered
2 carrots, scrubbed, sliced
¼ c. vegetable stock
Salt to taste

Cook pasta according to package directions, drain, and place in large pasta or mixing bowl. To prepare dressing, place vinegars, garlic, salt, and pepper in a blender and blend for 30 seconds. In a separate pot or skillet, sauté the broccoli, cauliflower, and carrots in the vegetable stock until al dente, approximately 6–8 minutes. Add artichoke hearts (drained) and three-bean salad (not drained), and heat for another 3 minutes. Transfer mixture to pasta and toss with dressing. If serving cold, chill in refrigerator for 3–4 hours.

Serves 6

EACH SERVING CONTAINS:
323 calories, 2 grams of fat, 10 grams of fiber.

Summer variation: use zucchini and yellow squash instead of broccoli and cauliflower; serve cold over a bed of baby greens.

Quinoa and Bell Pepper Salad

3 c. quinoa, prepared
3 scallions, chopped
1 red bell pepper, diced
1 yellow bell pepper, diced
2 c. garbanzo beans
1 c. shelled peas (Frozen peas that have been thawed work well.)
½ c. red wine vinegar
Salt and pepper to taste

Mix all ingredients. This can be served warm or chilled. Letting the flavors marry overnight is ideal but not necessary.

Serves 4

EACH SERVING CONTAINS:
244 calories, 1 gram of fat, 6 grams of fiber.

Soba-Grapefruit salad

Dressing
½ c. rice vinegar
2 tbsp. soy sauce
1 tbsp. agave nectar
¼ c. silken tofu
2 green onions
1 tbsp. ginger paste
1 tbsp. garlic paste
1 tsp. wasabi (or horseradish)

Put all ingredients in a blender and puree.

Salad
1 red bell pepper, thinly sliced
8 radishes, thinly sliced
5 green onions, sliced
6 oz. snow peas
2 c. red cabbage, shredded
2 beets, grated
1 pkg. tofu (firm, light), drained and cubed
2 grapefruit, sectioned and halved
1 pkg. soba noodles

Place firm tofu cubes onto cookie sheet lined with parchment paper and bake at 400°F for 30 minutes. Prepare soba according to package directions, drain, and cool in a large bowl. Toss in all vegetables (except beets), dressing, tofu, and grapefruit. When serving, top with shredded beets.

Serves 4

EACH SERVING CONTAINS:
344 calories, 3 grams of fat, 7 grams of fiber.

Asian Spinach Salad

12 oz. baby spinach
½ recipe Braised tofu (see Ginger Tofu and Julienned Vegetables with Noodles, page 134)
3 mandarin oranges, peeled and sectioned
1½ c. bean sprouts
½ lb. snow peas
1 red bell pepper, julienned
Wasabi Ginger Salad Dressing (see page 171)

On four large plates, divide spinach and top with sprouts, snow peas, pepper, tofu, and oranges. Drizzle dressing on top.

Serves 4

EACH SERVING CONTAINS:
323 calories, 4 grams of fat, 6 grams of fiber.

Sour Slaw

1 head green cabbage, washed and thinly sliced
5 carrots, washed and shredded
3 daikon watermelon radishes (or 1 medium daikon), washed, peeled, and shredded
1½ c. silken tofu
1/3 c. lemon juice
½ tsp. salt

In a blender, combine tofu, lemon juice, and salt. Place cabbage, carrots, and radishes in a large mixing bowl. Pour dressing over the top and toss. Refrigerate for 3–4 hours.

Serves 10

EACH SERVING CONTAINS:
51 calories, 1 gram of fat, 2 grams of fiber.

Sushi Salad

6 c. brown rice, prepared
1/3 c. rice vinegar
3 tbsp. agave nectar
1½ tsp. salt
6 sheets nori (seaweed)
2 cucumbers, peeled, seeded, and diced
1 c. pickled daikon
2 c. edamame (soy beans), shelled
½ c. pickled ginger
6 Red lettuce leaves

In a small bowl, combine vinegar, agave nectar and salt. Pour over brown rice and mix thoroughly. Tear nori into bite-sized pieces. Toss nori, daikon, edamame, ginger, and cucumbers into rice. Serve over red lettuce leaves.

Serves 6

EACH SERVING CONTAINS:
370 calories, 8 grams of fat, 9 grams of fiber.

Waldorf Salad

5 large Fuji apples, washed and diced
6 stalks of celery, washed and sliced
½ c. raisins
¾ c. orange juice
¼ c. silken tofu
1 tbsp. lemon juice

In a blender, combine tofu, lemon juice, and orange juice. Place apples, celery, and raisins in a large mixing bowl. Pour over salad and toss.

Serves 8

EACH SERVING CONTAINS:
36 calories, 3 grams of fat, 1 gram of fiber.

Soups

Add Fresh Fruits and Vegetables to Your Diet and Your Life

Increasing the number of fresh fruits and vegetables in our diets is a great way to get the vitamins, fiber, and phytonutrients we need. Growing food is also the most basic form of solar power—converting solar energy into calories we can use to fuel our bodies. Nothing compares to eating food straight out of your own garden, but not everybody has the time or space required for gardening.

Another way to get local fruits and vegetables is to sign-up for community supported agriculture (CSA) in your area. In programs like this, consumers subscribe to a service that deals directly with farmers. The CSA ensures that boxes of farm-fresh produce are delivered to their customer's doorsteps or to a central location in their neighborhood. If these services aren't available, consider going to a local farmer's market. Local, seasonal produce should require less energy to deliver goods to market. Produce grown in alternate hemispheres (e.g., buying peaches during the winter in the Northeastern United States) requires significant energy to get the goods to market.

Anytime Chili (Winter variation)

1½ c. kidney beans
1½ c. pinto beans
1 onion, chopped
5 cloves garlic, chopped
32 oz. diced canned tomatoes
2 c. broccoli stems, chopped
1 pkg. chili seasoning
6 oz. tomato paste
Salt to taste

Drain the tomato juice into a large pot and use it to sauté the onion and garlic for 3 minutes. Add the broccoli stems, chili seasoning, and tomatoes. Cook over medium heat for 7–8 minutes. Stir in the beans and tomato paste. Cook another 5–7 minutes, until heated through.

Serves 4

EACH SERVING CONTAINS:
295 calories, 1 gram of fat, 20 grams of fiber.

Summer variation: use zucchini instead of broccoli stems. Shorten the cooking time of the zucchini (to 4–5 minutes).

Asian Vegetable Soup

1 head bok choi, diced and leafy greens separated
1 onion, diced
¼ lb. snow peas, tips trimmed
1 carrot, thinly sliced
1½ c. bean sprouts
2 tsp. ginger paste
1 tbsp. garlic paste
10 oz. mushrooms, sliced
1½ c. seasoning soy sauce*
5 c. water
1 pkg. tofu (firm, light), drained and cubed
10 oz. soba noodles

Cook soba noodles separately according to package directions. Do not overcook. Drain in colander and set aside. In a large stockpot, add vegetables, ginger, garlic, mushrooms, seasoning soy sauce, and water. Bring to a boil. Cook until vegetables are al dente, approximately 5 minutes. Turn off heat and stir in soba noodles.

*Note: Seasoning soy sauce is not vegan; however, for the dietary intent of this cookbook, it adds no animal fat or protein to the dish. For vegan substitutions, consider 6 c. vegetable stock, no water, 2 tbsp. soy sauce, and 2 tbsp. agave nectar.

Serves 6

EACH SERVING CONTAINS:
340 calories, 4 grams of fat, 5 grams of fiber.

American Vegetable Soup

1 32 oz. can diced tomatoes + 1 can of water
1 lb. green beans, trimmed and cut into bite-sized pieces
3 carrots, peeled and sliced into coins
1 onion, diced
3 celery stalks, diced
2 bay leaves
1 lb. red potatoes, scrubbed, and diced
Salt and pepper to taste.

Place all vegetables and can of tomatoes in a large stockpot. Add 1 can of water. Bring to a boil and then simmer until vegetables are tender and potatoes easily fall off of fork, roughly 15–20 minutes. Salt and pepper to taste.

Serves 6

EACH SERVING CONTAINS:
151 calories, 0 grams of fat, 7 grams of fiber.

Butternut Squash Soup

2 leeks, cleaned and chopped
1 white onion, diced
1 stalk celery, chopped
1 carrot, washed and chopped
2 potatoes, peeled and diced
1 butternut squash, peeled, seeded, and diced
3 cloves garlic
5 c. vegetable stock
½ tsp. curry powder
Salt and pepper to taste

To clean leeks, wash the outside, cut off the roots and remove the tops approximately one-fourth of the way up the greens. Slice lengthwise and fan out the layers. Run water through the layers to remove all of the dirt before chopping. In a large pot, add vegetable stock and vegetables. Bring to a boil then simmer until the vegetables are tender, roughly 15–20 minutes. Add spices. Remove from heat and either transfer to a blender to puree or use an immersion blender until soup has a creamy texture.

Serves 8

EACH SERVING CONTAINS:
130 calories, 0 grams of fat, 6 grams of fiber.

Cabbage and White Bean Stew

1 onion, chopped
2 carrots, sliced
2 celery stalks, sliced
1 cabbage, diced
3 c. cannellini beans
3 c. vegetable stock
1 tbsp. agave nectar
2 c. canned, diced tomatoes
1 tbsp. cider vinegar
1 tsp. caraway seeds
Salt to taste

In a large pot, sauté onion with the juice from the canned tomatoes. Add carrots and celery. Sauté 3 more minutes. Add caraway seeds and cook for 1 minute. Stir in cabbage, vegetable stock, and agave nectar. Simmer 5 minutes. Stir in tomatoes with juice. Cover and simmer for 20 minutes. Add beans and vinegar. Cook until heated through and cabbage is tender.

Serves 8

EACH SERVING CONTAINS:
130 calories, 0 grams of fat, 8 grams of fiber.

Cabbage, Garbanzo Bean and Apple Stew

1½ lbs. Yukon gold potatoes, scrubbed and diced
½ head green cabbage, diced
2 granny smith apples, diced
1 onion diced
1½ c. (or 1 15 oz. can) garbanzo beans
4 cloves garlic, chopped
1½ qt. vegetable stock
2 tbsp. agave nectar
2 tbsp. mustard
1 tbsp. lemon juice
Salt and pepper to taste

Place all ingredients except garbanzo beans and cabbage in pot and bring to a boil. Turn down to medium heat and cook for 10 minutes. Add garbanzo beans and cabbage and cook until potatoes are tender, approximately 10–15 minutes more.

Serves 6

EACH SERVING CONTAINS:
269 calories, 1 gram of fat, 8 grams of fiber.

Celery Root and Rutabaga Soup

2 leeks, washed and diced (one-fourth of the way up the greens)
1 celery root, peeled and coarsely chopped
5 c. rutabaga, peeled and coarsely chopped
5 c. vegetable stock
3 c. almond milk, unsweetened
½ tsp. salt (optional)
1½ tsp. paprika
1 tsp. ground pepper
¼ c. lemon juice

To clean leeks, wash the outside, cut off the roots and remove the tops approximately one-fourth of the way up the greens. Slice lengthwise and fan out the layers. Run water through the layers to remove all of the dirt before chopping. Braise leeks in ½ c. of vegetable stock, stirring occasionally, until the leeks are tender, but not browned, about 5 minutes. Add the chopped rutabaga, celery root, and the remainder of stock. Simmer until the rutabaga is completely tender when pierced with a fork, about 30 minutes. Add the unsweetened almond milk, paprika, and pepper. Stir. Allow the soup to cool slightly, and then puree it in a blender until it is totally smooth. (You will have to do this in batches.) Alternately, you can use an immersion blender and puree. Taste and season with more salt and pepper as needed.

Serves 8

EACH SERVING CONTAINS:
96 calories, 1 gram of fat, 3 grams of fiber.

Fennel, Vegetable, and White Bean Stew

3 small fennel bulbs, washed and sliced
4 cloves garlic, chopped
1½ c. cannellini beans
1 tsp. rosemary
1 ½ tsp. oregano
½ tsp. salt
¼ tsp. black pepper
1 lb. asparagus, washed and cut into 1½ inch pieces
¾ c. white wine
2½ c. vegetable stock
8 oz. mushrooms, sliced
2 c. brown rice, cooked
Lemon wedges, to squeeze over the top

Prepare brown rice ahead of time. Pour ½ c. vegetable stock into large pot. Add fennel and garlic. Add beans, seasonings, wine, and 1 c. of vegetable stock and simmer for 15 minutes. Add mushrooms, asparagus and rice. Simmer 5–10 minutes, checking frequently so as not to overcook the asparagus. When pierced with a fork, the asparagus should cling briefly and fall off with a quick shake.

Serves 4

EACH SERVING CONTAINS:
315 calories, 2 grams of fat, 12 grams of fiber.

Fall variation: use broccoli (including the stems) instead of asparagus.

Summer variation: use zucchini instead of broccoli.

Gazpacho

3 cucumbers, peeled, seeded, and finely diced
2 red bell peppers, seeded, and finely diced
4 ripe tomatoes, finely diced
½ red onion, finely diced
12 oz. tomato-vegetable juice
½ c. red wine vinegar
¼ tsp. cayenne pepper
Salt to taste

Place all ingredients in a large mixing bowl and combine. Scoop out half of the mixture and place in blender or food processor and quickly pulse, keeping some texture to the mixture. Add blended vegetables back to the mixing bowl. Refrigerate overnight. Best served chilled.

Serves 6

EACH SERVING CONTAINS:
96 calories, 0 grams of fat, 2 grams of fiber.

Indian Daal

2 c. red lentils (daal)
8 c. of water
2 tsp. salt
1 onion, chopped
4 cloves garlic, chopped
1 tsp. turmeric powder
1 tbsp. mustard seeds

Wash lentils. In a large pot, boil water with salt, add lentils, onion, garlic, and spices. Cover pot and simmer for 2 hours, stirring occasionally. Lentils should be completely softened when done. Use an immersion blender to create a smoother soup.

Eat as a soup or ladle over brown rice.

Serves 6

EACH SERVING CONTAINS:
173 calories, 0 grams of fat, 15 grams of fiber.

Minestrone Soup

15 oz. diced tomatoes, Italian style
2 c. vegetable stock
16 oz. mixed frozen vegetables
15 oz. kidney beans
1 onion, diced
1 c. whole-wheat rotini pasta
Salt to taste

Cook rotini separately according to package directions. Do not overcook. Drain. Place mixed vegetables, tomatoes, onions and kidney beans in a large stockpot with vegetable stock and bring to a boil. Cook until onions are translucent. Turn off heat and stir in rotini.

Serves 4

EACH SERVING CONTAINS:
305 calories, 2 grams of fat, 14 grams of fiber.

Portuguese Greens and Beans Soup

2 leeks, washed and diced
1 onion, chopped
3 cloves garlic, chopped
15 oz. diced tomatoes
¼ c. lemon juice
1 qt. vegetable stock
3 carrots, scrubbed and sliced
3 potatoes, scrubbed and diced
1 bunch kale, washed and chopped (about 6 c.)
1½ c. cannellini beans
Salt to taste

To clean leeks, wash the outside, cut off the roots and remove the tops approximately one-fourth of the way up the greens. Slice lengthwise and fan out the layers. Run water through the layers to remove all of the dirt before chopping. In a large pot, add ½ c. vegetable stock, leeks, onion, and garlic. Sauté until slightly tender. Add diced tomatoes (not drained), lemon juice, remainder of vegetable stock, carrots, and potatoes. Bring to a boil, then turn down to simmer, approximately 20–30 minutes. When carrots and potatoes are tender, add kale and cannellini beans. Stir and cook another 5 minutes.

Serves 8

EACH SERVING CONTAINS:
196 calories, 0 grams of fat, 8 grams of fiber.

Sambar

2 c. red lentils
8 c. water
3 tbsp. tamarind concentrate
3 tbsp. sambar masala
1½ tsp. salt
1 onion, diced
20 oz. okra, cut into ½ inch lengths (or thawed frozen)
2 carrots, sliced

Wash lentils. In a large pot, boil water, add lentils, and then turn heat down to medium. Leave uncovered and cook until lentils are soft, roughly 2 hours. Mash lentils (or use immersion blender) and add seasoning and vegetables. Cook until vegetables are al dente and onions are translucent. This can be served as a thick stew or served over brown rice.

Serves 8

EACH SERVING CONTAINS:
162 calories, 0 grams of fat, 14 grams of fiber.

Main Dishes

Solar Cooking

Do you have an abundance of sunny weather? Does it ever get so hot you just don't want to cook in the house? If so, you might want to consider solar cooking. There are many variations on solar cooking. Anything that can be cooked in a slow cooker can be cooked in a solar oven. According to Shimeall, slow cooker recipes can be adapted for solar cooking by decreasing the amount of liquid and cooking time by two thirds. Recipes that call for conventional ovens can be generally be adapted by doubling the cooking time.[xxxvii]

Solar cooking works at lower temperatures, so it takes longer to prepare a meal. But if you have time on a hot summer day, it's an ecofriendly way to make dinner for the evening. Solar cookers can either be purchased or built with materials you may have sitting around the house.

Solar cookers have been used for years in developing countries to cook food and pasteurize water. More information can be found on the web by visiting www.solarcookers.org.

Anytime Green Enchiladas

3 c. brown rice, cooked
15 oz. corn, canned
1½ c. black beans
8 whole-wheat tortillas, burrito sized
1 onion, finely diced
28 oz. green enchilada sauce

Combine rice, corn, beans, and onion in a large bowl. Pour ½ of the enchilada sauce in the bottom of a 9x13 inch baking dish. Divide rice mixture into eight portions and roll into tortillas. Place enchiladas in baking dish. Cover with remaining sauce. Bake at 350°F for 25 minutes.

Serves 6

EACH SERVING CONTAINS:
340 calories, 6 grams of fat, 20 grams of fiber.

Bahn Mi with Seasoned Tofu

Seasoned Tofu
1 pkg. extra firm tofu, drained thoroughly
4 bulbs lemon grass
2 tbsp. soy sauce
3 cloves garlic
2 tbsp. agave nectar
2 tbsp. rice vinegar

Pickle
½ c. carrots, grated
½ c. daikon (or red radish), grated
2 tbsp. agave nectar
½ tsp. salt
½ c. rice vinegar

4 whole-wheat sandwich rolls
½ bunch cilantro, washed and coarsely chopped
Romaine lettuce leaves
1 fresh jalapeño pepper, thinly sliced (optional)

Preheat oven to 375°F. Slice tofu in half lengthwise. Turn each half on its side and slice lengthwise again into four even pieces. Combine lemon grass, 3 cloves of garlic, 2 tbsp. agave nectar, and 2 tbsp. rice vinegar in blender for 1 minute. Pour half of mixture into a shallow baking dish. Lay the tofu on the sauce, and then pour remainder of sauce on top. Bake tofu for 35 minutes. Meanwhile, combine grated carrot, daikon, 2 tbsp. agave nectar, salt, and rice vinegar in a bowl. Allow to sit while tofu is baking. Slice sandwich roles in half lengthwise (if not presliced). When tofu is ready, assemble sandwiches by placing lettuce, tofu, carrot/daikon pickle, cilantro, and optional jalapeños onto the bread.

Serves 4

EACH SERVING CONTAINS:
252 calories, 5 grams of fat, 6 grams of fiber.

Cabbage and Potato Wrap

¼ cabbage, sliced into ribbons ¼ inch wide
1 russet potato, scrubbed and diced ½ inch wide
1½ c. kidney beans
1 onion, finely diced
15 oz. canned tomatoes
1 bunch basil, coarsely chopped
1 sprigs fresh oregano, chopped
½ tsp. salt
1 tbsp. balsamic vinegar
8 whole-wheat tortillas, burrito size

Boil potato for 10–15 minutes or until tender. In a medium pan, sauté cabbage and onion with juice from the canned tomatoes and balsamic vinegar. Add tomatoes and kidney beans to cabbage and onion to heat through. Drain potatoes and add to vegetable mixture. Toss with herbs. Separate mixture into eight equal quantities and spoon one quantity into the center of each tortilla. To make the wraps, fold the edge of the tortilla closest to you over the mixture, then fold the sides toward the center, and then roll the tortilla away from you.

Serves 8

EACH SERVING CONTAINS:
139 calories, 1 gram of fat, 13 grams of fiber.

Calzones with Spinach and Tofu

1 loaf frozen whole-wheat bread dough, thawed
1 pkg. extra firm tofu, drained thoroughly
16 oz. frozen spinach, thawed and water squeezed out
1 c. pizza sauce (nonfat)
¼ c. whole-wheat flour for rolling out dough

Divide bread dough into four balls. Form into flattened circles on floured breadboard. Crumble tofu into large mixing bowl. Mix in spinach and pizza sauce. Spoon mixture onto bread-dough circles, and leave room around the edge to seal the mixture inside. Using wet fingers, gently moisten the edges. Fold and shape into calzones. Press folded edges together with fork tines to seal. Place onto baking sheet and bake at 400°F for 20 minutes.

Serves 4

EACH SERVING CONTAINS:
480 calories, 9 grams of fat, 9 grams of fiber.

Cannellini Bean and Bulgur Wheat Burgers

Patties
3 c. cannellini beans
3 c. bulgur wheat, prepared
2 tbsp. soy sauce
1½ tbsp. ginger, crushed
1½ tbsp. garlic, crushed
2 tomatoes, sliced
Romaine lettuce leaves
2 tbsp. tomato (or mango chutney)
4 slices whole-wheat bread
4 whole-wheat buns

Toast bread until very dry and tear into pieces. Place toast, beans, bulgur wheat, soy sauce, ginger, and garlic into food processor and combine thoroughly. Form into four patties. Line a baking sheet with parchment paper. Place patties on sheet and bake at 350°F for 20 minutes. Build burgers with tomatoes, lettuce, and buns, using the chutney as the dressing.

Serves 4

EACH SERVING CONTAINS:
411 calories, 4 grams of fat, 24 grams of fiber.

Curried Vegetable Wrap

1 lb. red potatoes, diced
2 carrots, diced
½ head cauliflower, diced
1 onion, diced
2 tomatoes, diced
2 tsp. curry powder
¼ c. water
½ tsp. salt
¼ head red cabbage, finely sliced
¼ c. mango chutney
8 whole-wheat tortillas, burrito size

Pour water, curry and salt into a large skillet. Over medium-high heat, cook potatoes, carrots, cauliflower, onion, and tomatoes until potatoes are tender, approximately 15–20 minutes, stirring frequently. To assemble wraps, spoon 1½ tbsp. chutney onto tortilla, add some shredded cabbage and 1/8 of the potato mixture. Fold in top and bottom, and then fold one side over the mixture and roll into wrap. For picnics, wrap with aluminum foil to hold shape.

Serves 8

EACH SERVING CONTAINS:
161 calories, 1 gram of fat, 11 grams of fiber.

Falafel with Vegan Tzatziki Sauce

Falafel patties
3 c. dried chickpeas (garbanzo beans)
Water (enough to cover the chickpeas with at least 2–3 inches of water)
1 large onion
6 cloves garlic
4 tsp. cumin
2 tsp. coriander
2 tsp. salt
½ tsp. black pepper
Dash cayenne pepper
1 bunch cilantro, stems trimmed
1 bunch parsley, stems trimmed

Vegan Tzatziki Sauce
2 pkgs. silken tofu
¾ c. lemon juice
1 c. fresh dill
1 c. fresh mint
3 cloves garlic
3 tbsp. miso paste
½ tsp. cumin
1 large tomato, diced
1 large cucumber, peeled, seeded, and diced

4 whole-wheat pita bread rounds, cut in quarters

Place dried chickpeas in a large mixing bowl or pot and cover with an extra 2–3 inches of water. Soak 8 hours. Drain chickpeas. Preheat oven to 375°F. Place half of the chickpeas in a food processor with an S-blade. Puree beans for approximately 1–2 minutes. Transfer to a large mixing bowl. Place the other half of chickpeas in food processor with all of the other ingredients. Puree mixture for approximately 1–2 minutes. Add this mixture to the chickpeas in the mixing bowl and combine thoroughly. (Amount of ingredients processed will vary by food processor capacity.) Line a baking sheet with parchment paper. Form falafel patties by hand, shaping them to be approximately 2½ inches in diameter and ½ inch thick. Bake at 375°F for 12 minutes. Flip patties and bake for another 12 minutes. Set the oven to broil and brown the tops for 1 minute. Makes approximately 32 falafel patties.

To prepare the sauce, place tofu, lemon juice, dill, mint, garlic, miso paste, and cumin in a blender and combine until smooth. Pour sauce into large mixing bowl. Fold in tomato and cucumber.

Serve falafel with sauce and pita corners on the side.

Serves 8

EACH SERVING CONTAINS:
444 calories, 8 grams of fat, 22 grams of fiber.

Grilled Eggplant and Roasted Red Pepper Sandwiches

1 eggplant, sliced
1 12 oz. jar roasted red peppers
¼ c. balsamic vinegar
Loose-leaf spinach
8 slices whole-wheat bread (preferably double fiber), toasted
Salt to taste

Sprinkle salt over sliced eggplant and let it sweat for 30 minutes. Dress with balsamic vinegar and place on grill (or under broiler) for 5 minutes. Top with spinach (to lightly wilt) and red peppers to warm. Serve on toast.

Serves 4

EACH SERVING CONTAINS:
207 calories, 2 grams of fat, 16 grams of fiber.

Grilled Vegetable Fajitas

1 green bell pepper, sliced into strips
10 oz. sliced mushrooms
1 onion, sliced into strips
1 red bell pepper, sliced into strips
2 zucchini, cut in half and sliced into strips
1 pkg. fajita seasoning mix
8 whole-wheat tortillas, soft taco size (50 calories; 8 grams fiber per tortilla)
Prepared salsa, optional

In a large, nonstick skillet, sauté vegetables until tender, approximately 8–12 minutes depending on the size and depth of pan used. As water cooks out, add seasoning packet, tossing with vegetables while cooking finishes. Serve in tortillas.

Serves 4

EACH SERVING CONTAINS:
176 calories, 2 grams of fat, 18 grams of fiber.

Pita Sandwiches with Black Bean Hummus and Spinach

Black Bean hummus
1½ c. black beans (if canned: drained but not rinsed)
2 cloves garlic
½ c. green onions, chopped
¼ tsp. red pepper
1 tsp. paprika
1 tsp. cumin
½ tsp. coriander
Salt and pepper to taste

1 bunch spinach, washed thoroughly
4 pita breads

Combine all ingredients for hummus in food processor until smooth. Spoon into pita bread and add spinach.

Variation: for a lighter colored hummus, use cannellini or garbanzo beans. If using canned garbanzo beans, reserve and include approximately two tablespoons of the liquid from the can for a smoother consistency.

Serves 4

EACH SERVING CONTAINS:
168 calories, 0 grams of fat, 8 grams of fiber.

Southwestern Squash Casserole

2 red kuri squash (or 1 whole butternut squash)
8 corn tortillas (soft taco size)
1 bell pepper, seeded and diced
3 cloves garlic, chopped
1 tsp. mustard seeds
1 c. prepared salsa
1½ c. pinto beans
4 tbsp. lemon juice
Salt to taste

Cut squash in half and remove seeds. Bake in oven on a cookie sheet at 350°F for 50–60 minutes or until soft. Remove from oven and set aside to cool. In a nonstick skillet on medium-high heat, toast the mustard seeds for one minute. They may pop like popcorn. Add garlic, peppers and lemon juice. Sauté for 4–5 minutes. Scoop out red kuri squash, place in bowl, and mash. Mix in peppers, garlic, and ½ c. of salsa. Layer (from bottom to top) a 9 x 13 pan with half of squash mixture, 4 tortillas (torn into strips), the other ½ of the squash mixture, pinto beans, 4 tortillas, and salsa. Bake in oven at 350°F for 30 minutes.

Serves 6

EACH SERVING CONTAINS:
241 calories, 2 grams of fat, 9 grams of fiber.

Summer Rolls

Wraps
1 pkg. spring roll wrappers (rice paper)
4 oz. alfalfa sprouts
½ English cucumber, julienned into 5 inch long pieces
4 carrots, grated
1 c. red cabbage, grated
2 yams, medium sized, cut into French fries
1 red pepper, seeded and julienned
6 oz. spinach, fresh

Sweet and Sour Sauce
½ pineapple, diced
1/3 c. pickled ginger
1/3 c. rice vinegar
½ tsp. tamarind concentrate
1/8 tsp. cayenne pepper
1 tsp. soy sauce

To make the wraps:

Line baking sheet with parchment paper and bake the cut yams for approximately 30 minutes or until soft. Alternately, place the yam pieces on a microwave safe plate, and cook for approximately 6 minutes in the microwave.

Meanwhile, completely moisten a clean kitchen towel (preferably cotton linen, not terry cloth) and place it in the center of your workspace. Fill a large frying pan (or other shallow dish that will hold the rice papers) with room temperature water. Lay out all wrap ingredients for easy access around the workspace. Prepare a bowl of water for rinsing fingers as necessary while you work. Place a serving tray nearby for finished wraps, and splash a little water on the surface to prevent wraps from sticking.

To assemble the wraps, immerse 1 rice paper in the water for approximately 1 minute to soften. Remove from water and lay out flat on the moist kitchen towel. Layer roughly ¼ c.

loosely packed alfalfa sprouts, 1–2 pieces of cucumber, approximately 2 tbsp. carrot, a few strips of red cabbage, 1–2 pieces of yam, 1 piece of red pepper, and 4–5 leaves of spinach (stems pointed toward the middle of the wrap. To finish the wraps, fold the edge of the wrapper closest to you over the mixture, then fold the sides toward the center, and then roll the wrapper away from you. Using a very sharp knife, slice the wraps in half at a slight angle and place on tray.

To make the sauce, cut off top and bottom of pineapple. Cut off outer skin, removing the "eyes." Coarsely dice pineapple and put it into a food processor set-up with the S-blade. Add all other sauce ingredients and puree for approximately 1 minute. Serve on the side as a dipping sauce.

Serves 5

EACH SERVING CONTAINS:
289 calories, 0 grams of fat, 9 grams of fiber.

Onions in a Balsamic Vinegar Reduction with Hummus

2 yellow onions, julienned
¾ c. balsamic vinegar
12 oz. roasted red bell peppers

Chickpea Hummus Indian Style (see Dressings and Sauces)

Whole-wheat pita bread

Place onions and vinegar in skillet. Boil over medium heat until onions are softened and vinegar has been reduced, approximately 10–15 minutes. Spread hummus onto pitas and add onions and roasted bell peppers.

Serves 4

EACH SERVING CONTAINS:
212 calories, 0 grams of fat, 9 grams of fiber.

Tabouli and Garbanzo Bean Wraps

1 c. bulgur wheat
2 c. water
1 cucumber, peeled, seeded, and diced
2 tomatoes, diced (excellent with ripe brandywine tomatoes)
1 bunch green onions, diced
½ bunch parsley, coarsely chopped
2 cloves garlic, chopped
¼ c. lemon juice
½ tsp. salt
1½ c. garbanzo beans
6 whole-wheat tortillas

In a small pot, boil water; add bulgur wheat, cover, and simmer for 10 minutes or until water is absorbed. In a bowl, combine cucumber, tomatoes, onions, parsley, garlic, lemon juice, salt, and garbanzo beans. Allow bulgur wheat to cool a little then add to vegetable mixture. Cool in refrigerator. Separate mixture into six equal quantities. Spoon one quantity into the center of a tortilla. To make the wraps, fold the edge of the tortilla closest to you over the mixture, then fold the sides toward the center, and then roll the tortilla away from you. For picnics, wrap in foil to hold shape.

Serves 6

EACH SERVING CONTAINS:
298 calories, 3 grams of fat, 19 grams of fiber.

Tacos de Verano

1 onion, diced
6 cloves garlic, chopped
3 medium zucchini, diced
2 cobs corn, kernels removed
1½ c. black beans (drained if canned)
3 tomatoes, diced
2 tbsp. lime juice
½ tsp. salt
½ tsp. cumin
½ tsp. coriander
¼ tsp. cayenne pepper
1 bunch cilantro, chopped
10 corn tortillas

In a large nonstick pan, sauté onions, garlic, zucchini, and corn in 1 tbsp. of lime juice until onions are translucent and slightly browned, roughly 5–8 minutes. Add black beans, tomatoes, and spices and heat through, 3–5 minutes more. Toss in cilantro. Serve with corn tortillas.

Serves 5

EACH SERVING CONTAINS:
347 calories, 3 grams of fat, 12 grams of fiber.

Vegetarian Burgers

3 c. black beans
1 c. brown rice, prepared
1 onion, diced
1 tsp. garlic powder
½ c. whole-wheat flour
2 tsp. Worcestershire sauce (or soy sauce for vegans)
Salt to taste
Whole-wheat hamburger buns
1 tomato, sliced
4 leaves romaine lettuce

Combine all ingredients in a food processor until well mashed, roughly 1 minute. Form into balls and refrigerate for an hour. Form balls into patties. Heat nonstick griddle to 350°F. Cook for 8–10 minutes on each side or until heated thoroughly. Serve on buns with tomatoes and lettuce.

Serves 6

EACH SERVING CONTAINS:
368 calories, 4 grams of fat, 13 grams of fiber.

Veggie Pizza

Crust
1 c. lukewarm water
1 pkg. active, dry yeast
1 tsp. agave nectar
¼ tsp. salt
2 c. whole-wheat flour

Sauce
1 15 oz. can diced tomatoes, drained thoroughly
2 cloves garlic
1 tbsp. Italian seasoning

Toppings
½ c. nutritional yeast
½ c. olives, chopped
½ c. mushrooms, sliced
1 c. broccoli, chopped into small (½ inch) pieces
1 c. spinach, washed and chopped

Summer variation: use zucchini and fresh tomatoes instead of broccoli and spinach.

Combine all crust ingredients in food processor. Place a few tablespoons of flour on a large cutting board and spread to cover. Place dough from food processor onto floured board, and knead for 5–10 minutes and form into crust. Line a baking sheet (or pizza pan) with parchment paper. Place formed crust onto pan. Set in warm location and let rise for 1½ hours.

If you have a bread machine, pour water in bottom of bread pan, add flour and salt. Make a well with your finger around the mixing paddle. Pour yeast into well and pour agave nectar just outside of the well. Set the bread maker to the dough selection. Remove and use dough when machine has finished the processing cycle.

To make the sauce, press the liquid out of the canned tomatoes. Place tomatoes in food processor with garlic and Italian seasonings. Blend for 30 seconds or until the sauce has a mostly smooth consistency.

When the crust is ready, spread sauce on the top, then layer with the nutritional yeast and vegetables. Bake at 450°F for 20 minutes. Slice into eight pieces.

Serves 4

EACH SERVING CONTAINS:
319 calories, 8 grams of fat, 14 grams of fiber.

Vegetarian Burritos

2 zucchinis, diced
1 onion, diced
4 oz. mild green chilies, diced
2 large tomatoes, diced
½ tsp. cumin
¼ tsp. cayenne pepper
¼ tsp. black pepper
1½ c. black beans, mashed (or substitute with nonfat vegetarian refried black beans)
1½ c. pinto beans, mashed (or substitute with nonfat vegetarian refried pinto beans)
Salt to taste
6 whole-wheat tortillas, burrito size

In a nonstick pan, sauté zucchinis and onion with spices until al dente (4–5 minutes). Mix chilies with beans and heat in microwave for 5 minutes (or until heated through). Separate mixture into six equal quantities. Spoon one quantity of beans into the center of a tortilla and top with tomatoes and vegetables. To make the wraps, fold the edge of the tortilla closest to you over the mixture, then fold the sides toward the center, and then roll the tortilla away from you.

Serves 6

EACH SERVING CONTAINS:
230 calories, 2 grams of fat, 19 grams of fiber.

Verde Wraps

1½ c. frozen peas, thawed
1 onion, quartered
1 lemon, juiced (3 tbsp.)
Salt and pepper to taste
12 oz. roasted red pepper, julienned
1 cucumber, peeled, seeded, and diced
2 carrots, shredded
¼ head red cabbage, finely shredded
8 whole-wheat tortillas, burrito sized

In a food processor, combine peas, onion, lemon juice, salt, and pepper. Separate mixture into eight equal quantities. Spoon one quantity of peas into the center of a tortilla and top with red pepper, cucumber, carrots, and cabbage. To make the wraps, fold the edge of the tortilla closest to you over the mixture, then fold the sides toward the center, and then roll the tortilla away from you. Wrap with foil to hold its shape.

Serves 8

EACH SERVING CONTAINS:
135 calories, 1 gram of fat, 10 grams of fiber.

Winter Red Enchilada Casserole

1½ c. red enchilada sauce
6 low-fat, low-carbohydrate flour tortillas, soft taco sized (50 calories; 8 grams fiber per tortilla), torn into strips
6 medium sized russet potatoes, scrubbed (not peeled), and diced
½ c. almond milk
½ c. vegetable stock
2 celery roots, washed, peeled, and diced (½ inch cubes)
3 carrots, scrubbed, diced
2 c. broccoli, chopped (stems separated from florets)
½ tsp. salt

Boil potatoes in salted water for 20 minutes or until tender. Meanwhile, in a nonstick pan, sauté celery root, carrots, and broccoli in vegetable stock. When potatoes are ready, mash them, and add the almond milk and salt. Whip with electric beater for 1–2 minutes to make smooth. Fold sautéed vegetables into the mashed potatoes. Pour ½ c. enchilada sauce in the bottom of a 13 x 9 inch baking dish. Lay strips of tortillas over sauce in a single layer. Top with half of the potato mixture. Pour another ½ c. of enchilada sauce onto potatoes. Add another layer of tortillas and potatoes. Continue until contents are depleted. Bake at 350°F for 20 minutes or until bubbling.

Serves 8

EACH SERVING CONTAINS:
273 calories, 1 gram of fat, 12 grams of fiber.

Black Beans and Rice with Peach Salsa

3 c. black beans
4 c. brown rice, prepared
¼ c. orange chicken sauce (purchased)
1 onion, diced
6 oz. spinach
Peach salsa (see page 167)

In a large nonstick skillet, sauté onion until translucent. Add black beans and orange sauce. Divide spinach onto four plates, and top with rice, black beans, and peach salsa (one recipe divided by four).

Serves 4

EACH SERVING CONTAINS:
254 calories, 1 gram of fat, 10 grams of fiber.

Braised Bok Choi with Beans

1 bunch bok choi, washed and diced (stems and leaves separated)
¼ c. vegetable stock
1½ tsp. ginger, grated
2 tsp. garlic, chopped
1 tbsp. soy sauce
1½ c. cannellini beans
4 c. brown rice, cooked

In a large, nonstick pan, sauté garlic and ginger in vegetable stock for 1 minute. Add bok choi stems. Cook for 3 minutes, and then add bok choi leaves and beans. Cover and simmer until stems are al dente and leaves are wilted, roughly 3 minutes. Serve over rice.

Serves 4

EACH SERVING CONTAINS:
313 calories, 0 grams of fat, 10 grams of fiber.

Bulgur Wheat with Mushrooms and Edamame

2 c. bulgur wheat
4 c. water
10 oz. shiitake mushrooms, sliced
1 onion, diced
1 ½ tbsp. black bean sauce (purchased)
2 c. soybeans, shelled

In a stockpot or large sauce pan, boil water, add bulgur wheat, cover, and turn heat down to simmer. Cook for 10 minutes or until water is absorbed. In a large nonstick wok, sauté onion and mushrooms until translucent, approximately 5–7 minutes. Stir frequently. Add soybeans to heat through, cooking for 2–3 minutes. Mix in cooked bulgur wheat. Stir in black bean sauce.

Serves 4

EACH SERVING CONTAINS:
423 calories, 9 grams of fat, 20 grams of fiber.

Creamy Pumpkin Curry

Sauce
1 pkg. silken tofu
6 oz. tomato paste
¾ c. pumpkin, pureed
1½ tsp. curry powder
4 cloves garlic, chopped
½ onion, chopped
1 c. water
Salt to taste

Vegetable balls
3 c. cannellini beans
2 tbsp. powdered egg replacer
½ c. water
1 onion, finely diced
2 tbsp. garlic
1 tsp. ginger, crushed
½ tsp. salt
¾ c. pumpkin, pureed
5 slices whole-wheat bread, toasted and torn

6 c. quinoa, cooked

Summer variation: use yellow squash instead of pumpkin.

To make the sauce, place tofu, tomato paste, pumpkin, curry, garlic, onion, and water in a blender or food processor and puree.

To make the vegetable balls, drain the cannellini beans (if canned). In a food processor, using the S-blade, mix cannellini beans, egg replacer, water, onion, garlic, ginger, salt, pumpkin, and toast for approximately 1–2 minutes, or until mixture is well combined but still retains some texture. Spoon onto baking sheets lined with parchment paper and bake at 400°F for 25–30 minutes.

Place 1 c. of quinoa on each plate. Top with vegetable balls and curry sauce.

Serves 6

EACH SERVING CONTAINS:
499 calories, 6 grams of fat, 22 grams of fiber.

Cauliflower Curry

1 large head cauliflower, washed, and chopped
1 potato, washed (not peeled) and diced
¼ c. vegetable stock
2 tsp. curry powder
1 clove garlic, minced or crushed
1 onion, diced
1 tsp. salt
1¼ c. water
1 c. diced tomato (canned)
2 tbsp. lemon juice
4 c. brown rice, cooked

Boil potato in salted water for 15 minutes. Sauté garlic and onions in vegetable stock over medium heat, stirring constantly, for 3–4 minutes. Add curry powder and cauliflower, and stir continuously for 5 minutes. Add the salt and water and cover the pan tightly. Allow the curry to simmer, covered, for 5 minutes. Add the potato, stir, cover again and leave to simmer for 10 minutes. Then add the tomato and lemon juice and stir, uncovered over medium heat, for another few minutes before serving.

Serves 4

EACH SERVING CONTAINS:
328 calories, 0 grams of fat, 7 grams of fiber.

Fruit and Pepper Medley

¼ c. lemon juice
1½ tsp. cumin seeds
1 tbsp. agave nectar
1 onion
5 cloves garlic
1 tbsp. ginger paste (or ground ginger)
½ c. mint leaves
1 yellow bell pepper, diced
1 red bell pepper, diced
1 green bell pepper, diced
2 nectarines, diced
3 apricots, diced
1 pkg. tofu (light, firm), cubed and baked
Salt to taste or serve with light soy sauce on the side
4 c. cooked brown rice

Cube 1 pkg. of light, firm tofu and place on a parchment paper-lined cookie sheet. Bake at 350°F for 45 minutes. In a dry nonstick skillet, toast cumin seeds on medium heat until color changes a bit. Add garlic and onion; cook until onions are translucent and just beginning to caramelize. Transfer to food processor or blender and add lemon juice, agave nectar, mint, and ginger. In a dry nonstick skillet, sauté bell peppers for 3–4 minutes, then add puree, fruit, and tofu. Heat through for 2–3 minutes, being careful not to overcook and reduce the fruit. Serve over brown rice.

Serves 4

EACH SERVING CONTAINS:
401 calories, 5 grams of fat, 7 grams of fiber.

Leeks, Mushrooms, and Kidney Beans in a White Wine Sauce

2 leeks, sliced lengthwise, washed, and thinly sliced crosswise
10 oz. mushrooms, sliced
4 celery stalks, diced
1 onion, diced
1 lemon, juiced
15 oz. diced tomatoes, Italian style
1 c. white wine
½ tsp. salt
¼ tsp. black pepper
¼ c. nutritional yeast
1½ c. kidney beans
1 tbsp. cornstarch
6 c. brown rice, cooked

To clean leeks, wash the outside, cut off the roots and remove the tops approximately one-fourth of the way up the greens. Slice lengthwise and fan out the layers. Run water through the layers to remove all of the dirt before chopping. In a large, nonstick skillet, sauté leeks, celery, mushrooms, and onion in wine and lemon juice for 5–7 minutes. Add tomatoes, salt, pepper, nutritional yeast, and kidney beans. Mix cornstarch with 2 tbsp. of water. Pour into pan and let sauce thicken, cooking for 3–5 more minutes. Serve over rice.

Serves 6

EACH SERVING CONTAINS:
468 calories, 2 grams of fat, 15 grams of fiber.

Mediterranean Beans and Rice

2 c. kidney beans
4 c. brown rice, cooked
3 oz. sun-dried tomatoes, julienne
12 oz. spinach, washed and large stems removed
¼ + ½ c. white wine
3 cloves of garlic, chopped
¼ c. nutritional yeast
2 tbsp. balsamic vinegar
Salt and pepper to taste

Soak the dried tomatoes in ½ c. of white wine overnight in the refrigerator. (If you are short on time, place tomatoes and wine in a microwave safe dish and heat for 2 minutes.) In a large pot over medium heat, sauté garlic for 2 minutes in ¼ c. of white wine. Add kidney beans, brown rice, nutritional yeast, and rehydrated tomatoes. Stir frequently to prevent burning. Heat until ingredients are warmed through, then stir in spinach. Cook until the leaves are just wilted.

Serves 6

EACH SERVING CONTAINS:
291 calories, 2 grams of fat, 10 grams of fiber.

Stuffed Sweet Dumpling Squash (or Peppers)

4 sweet dumpling squash, washed, top sliced off, and seeds removed
1½–2 c. brown rice, prepared
½ onion, finely diced
3 cloves garlic, chopped
½ c. white wine
1½ c. kidney beans
1 tsp. crushed rosemary
Salt and pepper to taste

Bake squash shells in oven at 350°F for 40 minutes. In the meantime, sauté onion, garlic, and rosemary in the white wine. Mix in rice and beans. Season with salt and pepper. Scoop stuffing into squash. Bake for another 20 minutes.

Serves 4

EACH SERVING CONTAINS:
267 calories, 1 gram of fat, 13 grams of fiber.

Summer variation: stuff yellow, red, orange, or green bell peppers instead. (Do not pre-bake the peppers.)

Vegetarian Jambalaya

1 onion, diced
1 green bell pepper, diced
2 cloves garlic, chopped
2 15 oz. cans diced tomatoes
1½ c. kidney beans
1½ c. pinto beans
¼ c. Worcestershire sauce (or soy sauce for vegans)
3 tbsp. lemon juice
¼ tsp. cayenne pepper
½ tsp. thyme
1 c. quinoa
2/3 c. water

Place all ingredients in a large stockpot and bring to a boil, then cover and simmer for 15 minutes or until quinoa is fully cooked.

Serves 4

EACH SERVING CONTAINS:
411 calories, 2 grams of fat, 19 grams of fiber.

Zucchini and Garbanzo Beans

1 onion, chopped
4 zucchini, diced
1½ c. garbanzo beans
1 c. vegetable broth
¼ tsp. turmeric
¼ tsp. cumin
3 cloves garlic, chopped
3 oz. sun-dried tomatoes
1 tsp. flour
Salt to taste
3 c. bulgur wheat, prepared

In a large pot, combine onion, zucchini, beans, broth, turmeric, cumin, garlic, and tomatoes. Simmer 7 minutes, until zucchini is almost tender. Mix in flour to thicken sauce. Cook another 3 minutes. Serve over bulgur wheat.

Serves 4

EACH SERVING CONTAINS:
345 calories, 3 grams of fat, 17 grams of fiber.

Chaat with Garbanzo Beans and Melon

2 lbs. red potatoes, scrubbed (not peeled) and diced
1½ c. garbanzo beans
½ red onion, diced
½ cantaloupe or honeydew melon, diced
½ bunch cilantro, diced
4 stalks of celery, diced
1 tbsp. chaat masala (or substitute with curry powder)
1 c. Tamarind Date Chutney (See Chapter 8)
Crisped rice cereal (purchased box cereal, ¼ c. per serving)
Salt to taste

In a large stockpot, boil potatoes for 20 minutes or until tender. Drain. In a large mixing bowl, combine all ingredients. When serving, sprinkle the top with the crisped rice cereal.

Serves 6

EACH SERVING CONTAINS:
490 calories, 2 grams of fat, 12 grams of fiber.

Fassolakia Ladera

1 onion, diced
1 lb. fresh green beans, tips and tails trimmed
2 zucchini, diced
1 lb. red potatoes, scrubbed and diced
1 bunch parsley, coarsely chopped
28 oz. canned tomatoes, Italian style
½ c. white wine
Salt and pepper to taste

Add all ingredients to a large pot and bring to a boil. Cover and cook over medium heat for 20 minutes or until vegetables are tender.

Serves 4

EACH SERVING CONTAINS:
245 calories, 0 grams of fat, 12 grams of fiber.

Indian Beet Burgers

3 c. beets, grated
3 c. carrots, grated
1 c. onion, finely chopped
5 cloves garlic, finely chopped
3½ tbsp. egg replacer + ¾ c. water
2 tbsp. ginger paste
¼ c. apple cider vinegar
1 tsp. turmeric
1 tsp. salt
½ c. whole-wheat flour

Mix all ingredients in large bowl. Line two baking sheets with parchment paper. Form 10 ½ inch thick patties on baking sheets. Bake at 350°F for 40 minutes.

Serves 5

EACH SERVING CONTAINS:
194 calories, 0 grams of fat, 5 grams of fiber.

Potato and Pepper Casserole

6 cloves garlic
2 tsp. paprika
1 bunch fresh cilantro
4 tbsp. lemon juice
3 tbsp. red wine vinegar
2 lbs. red potatoes, scrubbed and diced
1 yellow bell pepper
1 green bell pepper
1 red bell pepper
4 stalks celery, diced
3 tomatoes, diced
1½ c. garbanzo beans
Salt to taste

In a food processor, combine garlic, paprika, cilantro, lemon juice, and vinegar. Place potatoes, pepper, celery, tomatoes, and garbanzo beans in a large bowl and toss with cilantro mixture. Put mixture into a large baking dish and bake at 350°F for 50–60 minutes or until potatoes are cooked through.

Serves 6

EACH SERVING CONTAINS:
292 calories, 1 gram of fat, 8 grams of fiber.

Simple Potato Bajji

2 lbs. red potatoes, scrubbed and diced
1 onion, diced
1 green bell pepper, diced
1½ c. peas, thawed
1 lemon, juiced (3 tbsp.)
3 curry leaves* (found at Indian grocery store)
1 tsp. mustard seeds
¼ tsp. cumin seeds
½ tsp. turmeric
½ tsp. salt (or to taste)

In a large stockpot, boil potatoes for 15–20 minutes until tender and drain. In large skillet, sauté onion, bell pepper, and spices in half of the lemon juice for 5 minutes and add peas. Heat thoroughly, roughly 3–5 minutes. In a large bowl, combine mixture with potatoes. This is best served with Mint Chutney (see Chapter 8 Dressings and Sauces).

* Substitute with bay leaves if curry leaves are not available.

Serves 4

EACH SERVING CONTAINS:
360 calories, 0 grams of fat, 9 grams of fiber.

Sambar Potato Bajji

2 lbs. red potatoes, diced
1 onion, diced
¼ c. lemon juice
1 tbsp. sambar masala
6 oz. fresh spinach
Salt and pepper to taste

In a large stockpot, boil potatoes in water for approximately 15 minutes or until tender. In a dry nonstick skillet, sauté onion and add lemon juice as onions become translucent. Drain potatoes and transfer back into pot. Add onions, sambar masala, spinach, salt, and pepper. Place back on medium heat and cook until spinach is wilted, just a couple of minutes. Stir constantly to prevent burning.

Serves 4

EACH SERVING CONTAINS:
237 calories, 0 grams of fat, 7 grams of fiber.

Spaghetti Squash and Vegetables

1 spaghetti squash, washed, cut lengthwise, and seeded
3 tbsp. vegetable stock
1 onion, chopped
2 tbsp. garlic, chopped
3 oz. sun-dried tomatoes
3 carrots, scrubbed and sliced
3 celery stalks, washed and diced
1 bunch spinach, washed and chopped
1½ c. kidney beans
1 c. white wine
Salt and pepper to taste

Bake squash face down for 1 hour at 375° F. In a glass bowl, soak sun-dried tomatoes in white wine. Set aside. Sauté onion, garlic, carrots, and celery in vegetable stock until softened. Add kidney beans until heated through. Once squash is baked, let cool until it can be handled comfortably and "comb" out the strands with a fork. Place contents in large bowl. Add all other ingredients and combine.

Serves 6

EACH SERVING CONTAINS:
186 calories, 0 grams of fat, 11 grams of fiber.

Sloppy Joes

3 stalks celery, cut lengthwise, then diced
1 carrot, peeled and diced
1 onion, diced
1½ c. kidney beans
1 c. brown rice, cooked
¼ tsp. salt
3 tbsp. barbecue sauce
2 tbsp. lemon juice
4 medium yams, scrubbed (not peeled)

Pierce yams with fork and bake at 375°F for 50–60 minutes or until soft. Meanwhile, in a large nonstick skillet, sauté celery, carrots, and onion for 5–7 minutes, or until onion is translucent and starting to caramelize. Stir in kidney beans, rice, salt, barbecue sauce, and lemon juice, and heat through, cooking another 5 minutes. Turn heat down to simmer while yams finish cooking. When yams are done, cut a 2–3 inch slice into the top and press into the sides with your fingers to mash open. Top yams with Sloppy Joes mixture.

Serves 4

EACH SERVING CONTAINS:
463 calories, 1 gram of fat, 18 grams of fiber.

Tamale Casserole

2 zucchinis, diced
10 oz. mushrooms, sliced
1 onion, diced
2 carrots, thinly sliced
1½ c. black beans
1 pkg. fajita seasoning mix
1 8.5 oz. pkg. corn bread mix

Toss zucchini, mushrooms, onion, carrots, and black beans in a large bowl with fajita seasoning. Mix corn bread dough according to package directions. Line a 13 x 9 inch baking dish with parchment paper. Bake at 350°F for 30–40 minutes, or until a knife inserted into corn bread comes out clean.

Serves 6

EACH SERVING CONTAINS:
260 calories, 4 grams of fat, 7 grams of fiber.

Winter variation: use broccoli instead of zucchini.

Teriyaki Vegetable Croquettes

2 zucchinis, sliced ¼ inch thick
2 yellow squash, sliced ¼ inch thick
2 Japanese eggplants, sliced ¼ inch thick
2 onions, halved and then quartered
8 oz. mushrooms
Skewers
½ c. light teriyaki sauce, bottled

Alternate vegetables on skewers until all of the vegetables have been used up. Barbeque or broil 10–15 minutes or until vegetables are al dente. Meanwhile, warm the sauce on the stove. When serving, pour sauce over croquettes.

Serves 4

EACH SERVING CONTAINS:
91 calories, 0 grams of fat, 3 grams of fiber.

Zucchini Pancakes

5 medium zucchini, grated
2 carrots, grated
1 onion, finely diced
3 tbsp. powdered egg replacer
3/4 c. water
½ tsp. salt
¼ tsp. black pepper
½ c. whole-wheat flour

Combine zucchini, carrots, and onion in a large bowl. In a separate bowl, combine egg replacer, water, salt, pepper, and flour. Add mixture to vegetables and mix thoroughly. Heat a nonstick griddle to 350° F. Spoon mixture onto griddle into 4–5 inch diameter pancakes. Cook for 5–7 minutes per side, until center is not runny.

Serves 4

EACH SERVING CONTAINS:
93 calories, 0 grams of fat, 4 grams of fiber.

Ginger Tofu and Julienned Vegetables with Noodles

Braised tofu
1 c. apple juice
¼ c. ginger, pureed
¼ c. garlic, chopped
½ c. low sodium soy sauce
½ c. agave nectar
2 pkgs. extra firm tofu, sliced in half crosswise, then into ½ inch wide strips

Mix apple juice, ginger, garlic, soy sauce, and agave nectar. Pour a quarter of the mixture into the bottom of a 9 x 13 inch baking pan. Pour another quarter into the bottom of a second 9 x 13 inch baking pan. Arrange the tofu strips in a single layer. Pour remaining braising liquid over the tofu. Bake at 350°F for 50 minutes.

Julienned vegetables
2 broccoli heads, julienned stems and small florets
5 large carrots, julienned
1 large onion, julienned
¼ c. apple juice
¼ c. soy sauce
2 tsp. ginger, pureed
2 tsp. garlic, pureed

In a large wok or nonstick skillet, stir fry the vegetables, ginger, and garlic in the apple juice and soy sauce for approximately 4–5 minutes, or until al dente.

Noodles
14 oz. whole-wheat linguine (or soba noodles)

Break pasta in half and prepare according to package directions. Toss julienned vegetables into pasta and serve with strips of tofu on top.

Serves 6

EACH SERVING CONTAINS:
678 calories, 9 grams of fat, 17 grams of fiber.

Eggplant with Tomatoes, Onion, and Mint

3 Japanese eggplants, diced
1 red onion, sliced
4 tomatoes, diced
8 oz. bamboo shoots
3 tbsp. agave nectar
2 tbsp. soy sauce, low sodium
1 tbsp. lime juice
2 tsp. garlic paste
1/8–1/4 tsp. cayenne pepper
1 bunch mint
3 c. bean sprouts
1 14 oz. whole-wheat linguine (or soba noodles)

Prepare pasta according to package directions and drain. Sauté eggplant and onion over medium heat for 7–10 minutes. In a blender, combine agave nectar, soy sauce, lime juice, garlic paste, cayenne pepper, and mint. Pour over eggplant and onions. Toss in tomatoes and bamboo shoots and heat through. Do not overcook the tomatoes. They should retain their shape. To serve, put pasta on the plate, then top with bean sprouts and vegetable mixture.

Serves 4

EACH SERVING CONTAINS:
390 calories, 1 gram of fat, 13 grams of fiber.

Mushroom Stroganoff

16 oz. sliced mushrooms
3 c. unsweetened almond milk
2 tbsp. cornstarch
¼ c. nutritional yeast
1½ onions, diced
3 cloves garlic, chopped
¾ c. white wine
2 tbsp. Worcestershire sauce
14 oz. whole-wheat "eggless" noodles
Salt and pepper to taste

In a blender, combine almond milk, nutritional yeast, and cornstarch. In a large pot, boil noodles according to package directions. Meanwhile, in a large, nonstick skillet, sauté the onions, garlic, and mushrooms in ¼ c. of white wine for 5–7 minutes or until onion is translucent. If necessary, drain off the excess fluid or remove with a large spoon. Add the almond milk mixture, remaining wine, and Worcestershire sauce, and simmer for 5 minutes or until sauce thickens. Serve over noodles.

Serves 4

EACH SERVING CONTAINS:
439 calories, 4 grams of fat, 13 grams of fiber.

Pasta Verde

1 onion, chopped
4 cloves garlic, chopped
1½ c. vegetable stock
2/3 c. lemon juice
1 large head broccoli, chopped and florets separated
1½ c. frozen peas
1 bunch basil leaves
½ tsp. salt
½ tsp. black pepper, ground
1 16 oz. pkg. whole-wheat pasta

Prepare pasta according to directions. In a separate pot, boil onion, garlic, and broccoli stems in vegetable stock and lemon juice until stems are tender. Add frozen peas and cook until heated through, trying to retain the bright green color of the peas. Transfer all contents to a blender or food processor. Add basil, salt, and pepper to mixture and puree. In a separate pot or steamer, cook florets until al dente. Ladle sauce over pasta and top with florets.

Serves 6

EACH SERVING CONTAINS:
557 calories, 3 grams of fat, 17 grams of fiber.

Spring variation: use asparagus instead of broccoli.

Pasta with Lemon, Peppers, and Peas

13.25 oz. whole-wheat farfalle pasta (bow ties)
1½ c. frozen peas
½ c. lemon juice
½ tsp. black pepper
¼ tsp. cayenne pepper
12 oz. roasted red peppers, drained and julienned
½ red onion, diced
Salt to taste

Soak red onion in lemon juice and black pepper overnight. Prepare pasta according to package directions. In a medium skillet, heat onion in lemon juice, red peppers, and peas. Transfer pasta and vegetable mixture to a large bowl and toss together. Add more lemon juice, pepper or salt to taste.

Serves 4

EACH SERVING CONTAINS:
443 calories, 2 grams of fat, 13 grams of fiber.

Pearl Couscous with Cherries and Apricots

1 c. whole-wheat pearl couscous
2 c. water
1 c. cherries, pitted and halved
1 c. apricots, pitted and diced
1 bunch parsley, chopped
1½ c. garbanzo beans
4 stalks celery, diced
¾ c. lemon juice
¼ tsp. cayenne pepper
½ tsp. salt
½ tsp. turmeric

In a large saucepan, boil water, add couscous, cover, and turn heat down to simmer. Cook for 10 minutes, until water is absorbed. Meanwhile, toss all of the remaining ingredients in a large bowl. Add couscous. May be served warm or chilled.

Serves 4

EACH SERVING CONTAINS:
293 calories, 3 grams of fat, 10 grams of fiber.

Fall variation: use pomegranates and persimmons or apples instead of cherries and apricots.

Summer Vegetables Over Pasta (Ratatouille)

1 eggplant, diced
2 zucchini, diced
2 yellow squash, diced
1 onion, diced
4 tomatoes, diced
4 cloves garlic, chopped
1 bunch fresh basil, chopped
1 red bell pepper, diced
1 c. white wine
6 oz. tomato paste
Salt to taste
1 14 oz. pkg. whole-wheat rotini pasta, prepared according to package directions

Place diced eggplant in colander and toss with some salt. Let it sit for 30 minutes. In a large pot, sauté garlic, onions, and bell pepper in ¼ c. wine. Add eggplant, zucchini, squash, tomatoes, and the remainder of the wine. Cover and simmer until squash is tender. Stir in basil and tomato paste. Serve over pasta.

Solar cooker instructions: Instead of following the steps above, add all of the ingredients except the wine, tomato paste, and basil to a solar cooking container. (I use a black Dutch oven.) Set in the sun for 4–5 hours. Add the remaining ingredients, but cut the amount of wine to ¼ c. Prepare the pasta separately on the stove.

Serves 6

EACH SERVING CONTAINS:
140 calories, 0 grams of fat, 7 grams of fiber.
Whole-wheat rotini pasta 3.5 oz.: 368 calories, 3 grams of fat, 7 grams of fiber.

Whole-wheat Capellini Pomodoro

10 large tomatoes, ripened to perfection and diced
5 cloves garlic, chopped
1 bunch basil, chopped
¼ c. white wine
¼ c. red wine vinegar
Salt to taste
1 14 oz. pkg. whole-wheat angel hair pasta (thin spaghetti), prepared according to package directions

In a large nonstick skillet, sauté garlic in wine over medium heat. Add tomatoes, basil, vinegar, and salt. Cook for 3–5 minutes or until tomatoes are heated. Do not overcook. Tomatoes should retain their shape. Serve over pasta.

Serves 4

EACH SERVING CONTAINS:
303 calories, 2 grams of fat, 8 grams of fiber.

Side Dishes

Ditch the Car

Part of living a healthy life is getting the exercise we need. If you don't live too far from the store, consider leaving the car at home and walk or bike instead of drive. Doing so gives us two benefits: exercise and reducing our impact on the environment.

Corn Muffins

1½ c. cornmeal
½ c. whole-wheat flour
1 tbsp. baking powder
1 tsp. baking soda
1 tsp. salt
1¼ c. almond milk, unsweetened
2 tbsp. powdered egg replacer
½ c. water
1 15.25 oz. can corn (no sugar added)
1 4 oz. can mild green chilies, diced

In a large bowl, combine dry ingredients. In another bowl, combine the almond milk, egg replacer, and water. Add wet ingredients to the dry ingredients and combine thoroughly. Fold in corn (not drained) and green chilies. Spoon mixture into a nonstick muffin pan. Bake at 400°F for 15–20 minutes or until a knife inserted comes out clean.

Makes 12 muffins

EACH SERVING CONTAINS:
110 calories, 1 gram of fat, 3 grams of fiber.

Glazed Turnips

3 c. turnips, washed, peeled, and quartered
Water (as described below)
1 tbsp. agave nectar
Salt to taste

Arrange turnips in 1 layer in a large skillet and add enough water to cover them halfway. Add agave nectar and salt. Cover pot and boil over moderately high heat for 10 minutes, stirring occasionally. Uncover the skillet and continue boiling turnips, stirring occasionally, until they are tender and water has evaporated, about 8 minutes. Continue cooking turnips over moderately high heat until golden brown, about 5 minutes more. Add 3 tbsp. water and stir to coat turnips with glaze.

Serves 6

EACH SERVING CONTAINS:
24 calories, 0 grams of fat, 2 grams of fiber.

Kale with Onions

1 bunch kale, washed and chopped
1 onion, chopped
1 lemon, juiced (3 tbsp.)
1 c. diced tomato (canned)
3 tbsp. vegetable stock
1 tsp. black mustard seeds
Salt and pepper to taste

In dry nonstick skillet, heat mustard seeds until they pop, 1–2 minutes. Add vegetable stock and sauté onion until almost transparent, approximately 4–5 minutes. Add kale, lemon juice, salt, and tomatoes. Cover and simmer until greens are wilted.

Serves 4

EACH SERVING CONTAINS:
55 calories, 0 grams of fat, 4 grams of fiber.

Marinated Asparagus

1½ lbs. asparagus, tough ends trimmed off
¼ c. red wine vinegar
1 tsp. garlic powder
Salt and pepper to taste

In a large skillet, place asparagus spears in one layer and add enough water to cover them. Boil on high heat 5–7 minutes, depending on the thickness of the asparagus. Cook until al dente. To check, stick a fork into the asparagus. The spear should cling to the fork and fall off with a very gentle shake. Do not overcook. Drain asparagus and place in glass 13 x 9 inch dish. Sprinkle vinegar, garlic powder, salt, and pepper over the top. Let sit for at least 30 minutes. This can be served hot or chilled.

Serves 6

EACH SERVING CONTAINS:
29 calories, 0 grams of fat, 1 gram of fiber.

Mashed Rutabaga and Potatoes

3 rutabagas, peeled and diced
5 potatoes, scrubbed
2/3 c. almond milk, unsweetened
3 tbsp. vegetable stock
2 green onions, diced
1 tsp. salt
¼ tsp. black pepper

Boil rutabagas and potatoes in separate pots of water, as cooking time for each varies (approximately 20 minutes for potatoes and 30 minutes for rutabagas). Cook until soft. Drain. Meanwhile, sauté green onions in vegetable stock until soft. In mixing bowl, combine rutabagas, potatoes, onions, milk, salt, and pepper. Mash until mostly smooth. For smoother consistency, use electric mixer to finish.

Serves 6

EACH SERVING CONTAINS:
167 calories, 0 grams of fat, 4 grams of fiber.

Okra with Onions

1 lb. okra, sliced crosswise into ½ inch thick pieces
1 onion, diced
2 tomatoes, diced
¼–½ c. lemon juice
1 tsp. mustard seeds
Salt and pepper to taste

In a large dry nonstick skillet, toast mustard seeds for 1 minute, then add the vegetables. Cook over medium heat for 15 minutes. Add lemon juice and cook for another 10 minutes. Okra will shrink and become less slippery the longer it cooks.

Serves 4

EACH SERVING CONTAINS:
82 calories, 0 grams of fat, 6 grams of fiber.

Polenta with Chilies and Fresh Corn

2 c. water
1 c. corn meal
1 tsp. chili powder
½ tsp. salt
1 cob of sweet white corn, kernels sliced off
4 oz. mild green chilies, diced
½ c. nutritional yeast

In a medium saucepan, boil water. Add corn meal, chili powder, and salt, stirring with a wire whisk constantly. After 2 minutes, turn down to medium heat and continue to stir for 3–4 minutes. Once water is absorbed, the polenta should be the consistency of thick cream of wheat. Add fresh corn, chilies, and nutritional yeast. Continue to stir and cook for another 2 minutes. Pour into bowls. This is best served when topped with Anytime Chili (see Chapter 5 Soups).

Serves 4

EACH SERVING CONTAINS:
173 calories, 2 grams of fat, 6 grams of fiber.

Quinoa with Carrots and Lemon

1½ c. quinoa
3 c. vegetable broth
1 lemon, squeezed (3 tbsp. juice)
2 carrots finely chopped
½ tsp. salt

Boil water. Add quinoa, lemon juice, carrots and salt. Turn down to simmer and cover. Cook for 15 minutes or until water is absorbed.

Serves 6

EACH SERVING CONTAINS:
174 calories, 1 gram of fat, 3 grams of fiber.

Quinoa with Tomatoes and Chilies

1 c. quinoa
2 c. water
15 oz. can diced tomatoes
4 oz. mild green chilies, diced
½ tsp. salt

In a large saucepan, boil water. Add quinoa, tomatoes, chilies, and salt. Turn down to simmer and cover. Cook for 15 minutes or until water is absorbed.

Serves 4

EACH SERVING CONTAINS:
142 calories, 1 gram of fat, 4 grams of fiber.

Roasted Daikon with Mustard

4 daikon radishes, washed, peeled, and diced
2 tbsp. agave nectar
1 tbsp. Dijon mustard
Salt to taste

Line baking dish with parchment paper and add diced daikon. Bake at 350°F for 35 minutes or until soft. In small bowl, mix agave nectar and mustard. Drizzle over top of daikon and bake another 10 minutes or until daikon is soft.

Serves 4

EACH SERVING CONTAINS:
15 calories, 0 grams of fat, 1 gram of fiber.

Roasted Potatoes

6 medium potatoes, washed and diced
1 tbsp. Italian seasoning
Dash of salt and pepper

Line a baking sheet with parchment paper. Toss ingredients in a large bowl and then transfer to the baking sheet. Bake at 350°F for 50 minutes.

Serves 6

EACH SERVING CONTAINS:
212 calories, 0 grams of fat, 5 grams of fiber.

Sour Cabbage

1 head cabbage (green or purple), thinly sliced
1 onion, chopped
¼ c. vegetable broth
¼ c. lemon juice
¼ c. balsamic vinegar
¼–½ tsp. salt

In large skillet or pot (depending on the size of the cabbage), add broth and onion. Sauté for 4 minutes. Add cabbage, lemon juice, balsamic vinegar, and salt. Cover to steam cabbage. Stir frequently. Cabbage will be limp when cooking is finished.

Serves 6

EACH SERVING CONTAINS:
37 calories, 0 grams of fat, 2 grams of fiber.

Stuffed Mushrooms

12 large mushrooms
½ onion, very finely diced
½ slice dry, whole-wheat bread
Salt to taste

Toast bread at a medium-dark setting on the toaster. Toast should be dry enough to make breadcrumbs by crumbling the bread in your hands. Remove stems from mushrooms and dice the stems finely. Using a nonstick skillet, cook the mushroom stem bits and diced onion until onion is translucent and begins to caramelize. Sprinkle with salt. Crumble bread into breadcrumbs over pan, and stir into mushroom and onion mixture. Remove from heat. Place the mushroom caps in a microwave safe dish, and cook in the microwave on high for 3 minutes. Gently blot out any water from the middles of the mushroom caps. Stuff the caps with mixture of breadcrumbs, onion, and mushroom stems.

Serves 4

EACH SERVING CONTAINS:
39 calories, 0 grams of fat, 2 grams of fiber.

Swiss Chard with Balsamic Vinegar

1 bunch Swiss chard
1 onion, diced
1½ tbsp. balsamic vinegar

Separate the stems from the leaves of the Swiss chard. Dice the stems and sauté them with the onion for 3–4 minutes. Chop the leaves and add them to the pan. Add balsamic vinegar and cook until the leaves are gently wilted.

Serves 4

EACH SERVING CONTAINS:
37 calories, 0 grams of fat, 3 grams of fiber.

Tandoori Vegetable Skewers

2 zucchinis, sliced ¼ inch thick
2 yellow squash, sliced ¼ inch thick
2 Japanese eggplants, sliced ¼ inch thick
2 onions, halved and then quartered
8 oz. fresh mushrooms
Skewers
2 tbsp. tandoori masala
1 c. almond milk, unsweetened

Combine tandoori masala and almond milk. Toss vegetables with masala sauce and marinate in refrigerator for 30 minutes. Barbeque or broil 10–15 minutes or until vegetables are al dente.

Serves 4

EACH SERVING CONTAINS:
33 calories, 0 grams of fat, 2 grams of fiber.

Dressings and Sauces

Keeping it Clean and Green

Many detergents are made from fossil fuels, but good quality ecofriendly products are derived from plant sources. Switching to these products can help reduce our reliance on fossil fuels and be a more sustainable practice.

We can also reduce our use of energy by choosing to line-dry our linens instead of placing them in the dryer. When we switch away from using paper towels and napkins in the kitchen, we might do a little more laundry. In that case, kitchen linens are ideal for hanging outside to dry.

Chickpea Hummus (Indian style)

3 c. garbanzo beans (chickpeas)
½ tsp. salt
¼ tsp. cumin
¼ tsp. coriander
¼ tsp. paprika
½ tsp. garlic powder
½ tsp. curry powder
3 tbsp. rice vinegar
¼ c. lemon juice
¼ c. chopped cilantro (fresh)
2 tbsp. water or liquid reserved from canned beans
3 oz. sun-dried tomatoes, chopped into relish sized pieces

Combine all ingredients except the sun-dried tomatoes in food processor with S-blade and blend for 1–2 minutes, until hummus is creamy. Transfer to a large mixing bowl, and fold in sun-dried tomatoes.

Serves 8

EACH SERVING CONTAINS:
130 calories, 1 gram of fat, 5 grams of fiber.

Lemon Pepper Salad Dressing

1 c. lemon juice
2 tbsp. garlic paste
½ tsp. black pepper
¼ c. silken tofu
1 tbsp. miso paste

Combine all ingredients in a blender.

Serves 10

EACH SERVING CONTAINS:
28 calories, 1 gram of fat, 0 grams of fiber.

Mint Chutney

1 bunch mint, washed
6 green onions, coarsely chopped
4 oz. can mild green chilies
2 cloves garlic
1 tsp. salt
1 tsp. garam masala
2 tbsp. agave nectar
1/3 c. lemon juice
2 tbsp. water

Place all ingredients into a food processor and combine until smooth.

Serves 8

EACH SERVING CONTAINS:
23 calories, 0 grams of fat, 1 gram of fiber.

Peach Salsa

3 large peaches, peeled and diced
1 red onion, diced
1 lime, juiced
1 jalapeño, seeded and finely diced
¼ c. cilantro leaves, chopped
1 tsp. garlic paste
Salt to taste

Combine all ingredients in a bowl and refrigerate.

Serves 8

EACH SERVING CONTAINS:
35 calories, 0 grams of fat, 1 gram of fiber.

Tomato Salsa

4 roma tomatoes, diced
1 onion, finely diced
1 jalapeño, seeded and finely diced
1 lemon, juiced
½ bunch cilantro, chopped
¼ tsp. salt
3 cloves garlic, chopped

In a large bowl, mix all ingredients together. For a finer consistency, cut tomatoes and onions coarsely and add all ingredients to a food processor and pulse until all ingredients are combined.

Serves 6

EACH SERVING CONTAINS:
28 calories, 0 grams of fat, 2 grams of fiber.

Tamarind Date Chutney

8 dates, pitted
¼ c. tamarind concentrate
¼ c. water
1/8 tsp. cayenne pepper
½ tsp. cumin powder
1/8 tsp. black pepper
1 tsp. ginger

Combine all ingredients in a blender until smooth.

Serves 6

EACH SERVING CONTAINS:
98 calories, 0 grams of fat, 2 grams of fiber.

Vinaigrette Mustard Salad Dressing

½ c. balsamic vinegar
½ c. red wine vinegar
¼ c. agave nectar
3 tbsp. Dijon mustard
¼ tsp. black pepper

Combine all ingredients in a blender.

Serves 12

EACH SERVING CONTAINS:
21 calories, 0 grams of fat, 0 grams of fiber.

Wasabi Ginger Salad Dressing

½ c. concentrated, frozen apple juice, thawed
½ c. soy sauce, low sodium
½ c. rice vinegar
¼ c. silken tofu
2 tbsp. wasabi powder
1 tbsp. ginger paste
1 tbsp. garlic paste

Combine all ingredients in a blender.

Serves 25

EACH SERVING CONTAINS:
20 calories, 0 grams of fat, 0 grams of fiber.

Orange Miso Dressing

1 orange, peeled and seeded (if orange is not a seedless variety)
¼ c. rice vinegar
2 tbsp. miso paste
1 tsp. ginger, grated
1 clove garlic

Combine all ingredients in a blender for 1–2 minutes until smooth.

Serves 6

EACH SERVING CONTAINS:
20 calories, 0 grams of fat, 1 gram of fiber.

Index

Add Fresh Fruits and Vegetables to Your Diet and Your Life 71
American Vegetable Soup 74
Anytime Chili 72
Apple 49, 50, 68, 77, 140
Apricot and Peach Breakfast Cobbler 36
Apricots 36, 117, 140
Artichoke hearts 60, 62
Asian Spinach Salad 65
Asian Vegetable Soup 73
Asparagus 79, 138, 149
Bahn Mi with Seasoned Tofu 89
Bean Salad with Summer Vegetables 56
Beans, black 56, 88, 98, 104, 105, 108, 111, 131
Beans, black-eyed peas 56
Beans, cannellini 47, 76, 79, 83, 92, 112, 114
Beans, dried 30, 31
Beans, garbanzo 60, 63, 77, 94, 103, 122, 123, 126, 140, 164
Beans, green 74, 124
Beans, kidney 72, 82, 90, 118, 119, 120, 121, 129, 130
Beans, pinto 72, 99, 108, 121
Beans, soy (edamame) 50, 51, 67, 113
Beets 64, 125
Black Beans and Rice with Peach Salsa 111
Black Forest Smoothie 51
Blueberries 37, 41, 43, 51
Bok Choi 73, 112

Braised Bok Choi with Beans 112
Breakfast Burritos 47
Broccoli 62, 72, 79, 106, 110, 131, 134, 138
Buckwheat Blueberry Pancakes 37
Bulgur wheat 30, 31, 92, 103, 113, 122
Bulgur Wheat with Mushrooms and Edamame 113
Butternut Squash 38, 75, 99
Butternut Squash Soup 75
Butternut Squash Waffles 38
Cabbage 64, 66, 76, 77, 90, 93, 100, 101, 109, 157
Cabbage and Potato Wrap 90
Cabbage and White Bean Stew 76
Cabbage, Garbanzo Bean and Apple Stew 77
Calzones with Spinach and Tofu 91
Cannellini Bean and Bulgur Wheat Burgers 92
Cantaloupe 123
Carrot and Raisin Salad 57
Carrots 43, 51, 52, 57, 58, 62, 66, 73, 74, 75, 76, 83, 84, 89, 93, 100, 109, 110, 125, 129, 130, 131, 133, 134, 153,
Cauliflower 62, 93, 116
Cauliflower Curry 116
Celery 57, 68, 74, 76, 118, 123, 126, 129, 130, 140
Celery root 78, 110
Celery Root and Rutabaga Soup 78
Chaat with Garbanzo Beans and Melon 123
Chard 159
Cherries 49, 51, 140
Chickpea Hummus (Indian style) 102, 164
Chickpea Omelets 45
Chilled Noodle Salad with Peaches 58
Corn 56, 88, 104, 146, 152
Corn Muffins 146
Couscous 30, 31, 140
Cranberries 39
Cranberry Orange Bread 39

Creamy Pumpkin Curry 114

Cucumber 56, 58, 59, 61, 67, 80, 94, 95, 100, 101, 103, 109

Cucumber and Tomato Salad 59

Curried Rice and Artichoke Salad 60

Curried Vegetable Wrap 93

Daikon 66, 89, 155

Dates 51, 169

Ditch the Car 145

Eggplant 40, 96, 132, 136, 141, 160,

Eggplant with Tomatoes, Onion, and Mint 136

Eggplant "Sausage" Open-faced Breakfast Sandwiches 40

English muffins 40

Falafel with Vegan Tzatziki Sauce 94, 95

Fassolakia Ladera 124

Fennel 79

Fennel, Vegetable, and White Bean Stew 79

Five Simple Tips to Reducing Kitchen Waste 55

French Toast Casserole 41

Fruit and Pepper Medley 117

Garbanzo bean flour 45

Gazpacho 80

Gazpacho Salad 61

Ginger Tofu and Julienned Vegetables with Noodles 65, 134

Glazed Turnips 147

Grapefruit 64

Green Power Smoothie 50

Grilled Eggplant and Roasted Red Pepper Sandwiches 96

Grilled Vegetable Fajitas 97

Healthy Heart Apple Cake 42

High Protein Hot Cereal 48

Honeydew 123

Hot (or Cold) Pasta Salad 62

Indian Beet Burgers 125

Kale 50, 83, 148

Kale with Onions 148

Keeping it Clean and Green 163

Leeks 75, 78, 83, 118

Leeks, Mushrooms, and Kidney Beans in a White Wine Sauce 118

Lemon Pepper Salad Dressing 165

Lentils 48, 81, 84

Lettuce 61, 67, 89, 92, 105

Marinated Asparagus 149

Mashed Rutabaga and Potatoes 150

Mediterranean Beans and Rice 119

Minestrone Soup 82

Mint Chutney 127, 166

Mushroom Stroganoff 137

Mushrooms 73, 79, 97, 106, 113, 118, 131, 132, 137, 158, 160

Nectarine 52, 117

Noodles, soba 58, 64, 73, 134, 136

Oatmeal Raisin Breakfast Scones 44

Oatmeal, steel-cut 31

Okra 84, 151

Okra with Onions 151

Onions in a Balsamic Vinegar Reduction with Hummus 102

Orange Antioxidant Blast Smoothie 52

Orange Miso Dressing 172

Oranges 51, 52, 65, 172

Papaya 52

Pasta 62, 82, 134, 135, 136, 137, 138, 141, 142

Pasta Verde 138

Pasta with Lemon, Peppers, and Peas 139

Peach Salsa 111, 167

Peaches 111, 167

Pearl Couscous with Cherries and Apricots 140

Peas 63, 109, 127, 138, 139

Pepper, bell 46, 56, 60, 61, 63, 64, 65, 80, 96, 98, 99, 100, 101, 102, 109, 117, 120, 126, 127, 139, 141

Persimmon 140

Pineapple 100

Pita Sandwiches with Black Bean Hummus and Spinach 98
Planet-friendly Benefits of a Vegan Diet 23
Polenta with Chilies and Fresh Corn 152
Pomegranates 140
Portuguese Greens and Beans Soup 83
Potato 74, 75, 77, 83, 90, 93, 110, 116, 123, 124, 126, 127, 128, 150, 156
Potato and Pepper Casserole 126
Pumpkin 43, 114
Quinoa 30, 31, 63, 114, 121, 153, 154
Quinoa and Bell Pepper Salad 63
Quinoa with Carrots and Lemon 153
Quinoa with Tomatoes and Chilies 154
Radishes 64, 66, 89
Raisins 43, 44, 56, 57, 68
RhubAppleCherry Pancake Topper 49
Rhubarb 49
Rice, Brown 31, 60, 67, 79, 81, 84, 88, 105, 111, 112, 116, 117, 118, 119, 120, 130
Roasted Daikon with Mustard 155
Roasted Potatoes 156
Rutabaga 78, 150
Sambar 84
Sambar Potato Bajji 128
Scrambled Tofu 46
Seitan 58
Simple Potato Bajji 127
Sloppy Joes 130
Soba-Grapefruit salad 64
Sour Cabbage 157
Solar Cooking 87
Spaghetti Squash and Vegetables 129
Spinach 47, 51, 65, 91, 96, 98, 100, 106, 111, 119, 128, 129
Sprouts 58, 65, 73, 100, 136
Squash, red kuri 99
Squash, spaghetti 129
Squash, sweet dumpling 120

Stuffed Mushrooms 158
Stuffed Sweet Dumpling Squash (or Peppers) 120
Substitutions: Replacing Low Fiber Ingredients with Whole Grains 13
Summer Vegetables Over Pasta (Ratatouille) 141
Sushi Salad 67
Swiss Chard with Balsamic Vinegar 159
Tabouli and Garbanzo Bean Wraps 103
Tacos de Verano 104
Tamale Casserole 131
Tamarind Date Chutney 169
Tandoori Vegetable Skewers 160
Teriyaki Vegetable Croquettes 132
Tofu 40, 46, 57, 60, 61, 64, 65, 66, 68, 73, 89, 91, 94, 114, 117, 134, 165, 171
Tomato 40, 56, 59, 61, 72, 74, 76, 80, 82, 83, 90, 92, 93, 94, 95, 103, 104, 105, 106, 107, 108, 116, 118, 119, 121, 122, 124, 126, 129, 136, 141, 142, 148, 151, 154, 164, 168,
Tomato Salsa 168
Tortillas 47, 88, 90, 93, 97, 99, 103, 104, 108, 109, 110
Turnips 147
Vegetarian Burgers 105
Vegetarian Burritos 108
Vegetarian Jambalaya 121
Veggie Pizza 106
Verde Wraps 109
Vinaigrette Mustard Salad Dressing 170
Waldorf Salad 68
Wasabi Ginger Salad Dressing 171
Whole-wheat Capellini Pomodoro 142
Winter Red Enchilada Casserole 110
Yam 48, 100, 130
Yellow squash 43, 47, 62, 114, 132, 141, 160
Zucchini 43, 62, 72, 79, 97, 104, 106, 108, 122, 124, 131, 132, 133, 141, 160
Zucchini and Garbanzo Beans 122
Zucchini Pancakes 133

Endnotes

i   Murphy S.L., Xu J.Q., Kochanek K.D., "Deaths: Final data for 2010." *National Vital Statistics Report* vol. 61, no. 4 (2013).

ii   Enos W.F., Holmes R.H., Beyer J., "Coronary Disease among United States Soldiers Killed in Action in Korea." *JAMA* 152 (1953): 1090–1093.

iii   Joseph A., Ackerman D., Talley J.D. et al., "Manifestations of coronary atherosclerosis in young trauma victims—An autopsy study." *Journal of the American College of Cardiology* vol. 22, no. 2 (1993): 459–467.

iv   Strong J.P., Malcom G., McMahan A. et al., "Prevalence and Extent of Atherosclerosis in Adolescents and Young Adults: Implications for Prevention From the Pathobiological Determinants of Atherosclerosis in Youth Study." *Journal of the American Medical Association* vol. 281, no. 8 (1999): 727–735.

v   Ross R., "Atherosclerosis—An Inflammatory Disease." *New England Journal of Medicine* vol. 340 (1999): 115–49.

vi   Hambrecht R., Wolf A., Gielen S. et al., "Effect of Exercise on Coronary Endothelial Function in Patients with Coronary Artery Disease." *New England Journal of Medicine* vol. 342 (2000): 454–60.

vii   Tsai W.C., Li Y.H., Chao T.H. et al., "Effects of oxidative stress on endothelial function after a high fat meal." *Clinical Science* vol. 106, no. 3 (2004): 315–319.

viii Campbell T.C., Campbell T.M., Lyman H. et al., *The China Study* (Texas: Benella Books, 2006).

ix Ornish D., Scherwitz L.W., Billings J. et al., "Intensive Lifestyle Changes for Reversal of Coronary Heart Disease." *Journal of the American Medical Association* vol. 280, no. 23 (1998): 2001–2008.

x Ornish D., *Dr. Dean Ornish's Program For Reversing Heart Disease* (New York: Ivy Books, 1990).

xi Esselstyn C.B., Ellis S.G., Medendorp S.V. et al., "A Strategy to Arrest and Reverse Coronary Artery Disease: A 5-Year Longitudinal Study of a Single Physician's Practice." *The Journal of Family Practice* vol. 41, no. 6 (1995): 560–568.

xii Esselstyn C.B, "Updating a 12- Year Experience with Arrest and Reversal Therapy for Coronary Heart Disease (An Overdue Requiem for Palliative Cardiology)." *The American Journal of Cardiology* vol. 84, no. 6 (1999): 339–341.

xiii Esselstyn C.B. *Prevent and Reverse Heart Disease* (New York: Avery, 2007).

xiv Mishra S., Xu J., Agarwal U. et al., "A multicenter randomized controlled trial of a plant-based nutrition program to reduce body weight and cardiovascular risk in the corporate setting: the GEICO study." *European Journal of Clinical Nutrition* vol. 67, no. 7 (2013): 718–724.

xv Berkow S.E., Barnard N., "Vegetarian diets and weight status." *Nutrition Reviews* vol. 64, no. 4 (2006): 175–188.

xvi Heidenreich P.A., Trogdon J.G., Khavjou O.A. et al., "Forecasting the Future of Cardiovascular Disease in the United States: A Policy Statement from the American Heart Association." *Circulation* vol. 123 (2011): 933–44.

xvii Ogden C.L., Carroll M.D., Kit B.K. et al., "Prevalence of Childhood and Adult Obesity in the United States, 2011–2012." *Journal of the American Medical Association* vol. 311, no. 8 (2014): 806–814.

xviii Fryar C.D., Ervin R.B., "Caloric Intake from Fast Food Among Adults: United States, 2007–2010." NCHS data brief, no. 114. (Hyattsville, MD: National Center for Health Statistics, 2013).

xix Food and Nutrition Board, Institute of Medicine, National Academies, "Dietary Reference Intakes (DRIs): Estimated Average Requirements." Retrieved from: http://www.iom.edu/Activities/Nutrition/SummaryDRIs/~/media/Files/Activity%20Files/Nutrition/DRIs/EAR%20Table.pdf.

xx Institute of Medicine of the National Academies, "Dietary Reference Intakes for Energy, Carbohydrates, Fiber, Fat, Fatty Acids, Cholesterol, Protein, and Amino Acids." (Washington, D.C.: National Academies Press, 2005).

xxi Novick J., "The Myth of Complementary Protein." (June 3, 2013) Retrieved from: http://www.forksoverknives.com/the-myth-of-complementary-protein/.

xxii Ervin R.B., Ogden C.L., "Consumption of Added Sugars Among US Adults, 2005–2010." NCHS data brief, No 122. (Hyattsville, MD: National Center for Health Statistics. 2013).

xxiii "WHO opens public consultation on draft sugar guidelines." Retrieved from: http://www.who.int/mediacentre/news/notes/2014/consultation-sugar-guideline/en/.

xxiv Yang Q., Zhang Z., Gregg E. et al., "Added Sugar Intake and Cardiovascular Diseases Mortality Among US Adults." *JAMA Internal Medicine* vol. 174, no. 4 (2014): 516–524.

xxv Peterson N.D., Middleton K.R., Nackers L.M. et al., "Dietary self-monitoring and long-term success with weight management." *Obesity* vol. 10 (2014) (epub ahead of print).

xxvi Benson H., Klipper M., *The Relaxation Response* (New York: HarperCollins Publishers, 2000).

xxvii Kirkwood G., Rampes H., Tuffrey V. et al., "Yoga for anxiety: a systematic review of the research evidence." *British Journal of Sports Medicine* vol. 39, no. 12 (2005); 884–891.

[xxviii] West J., Otte C., Geher K. et al., "Effects of Hatha yoga and African dance on perceived stress, affect, and salivary cortisol." *Annals of Behavioral Medicine* vol. 28, no. 2 (2004): 114–118.

[xxix] 29 Selvamurthy W., Sridharan K., Ray U.S. et al., "A new physiological approach to control hypertension." *Indian Journal of Physiology and Pharmacology* 1998; vol. 42, no. 2 (1998): 205–213.

[xxx] Damodaran A., Malathi A., Patil N. et al., "Therapeutic potential of yoga practices in modifying cardiovascular risk profile in middle aged men and women." *Journal of the Association of Physicians of India* vol. 50, no. 5(2002): 633–640.

[xxxi] Bassett D., Wyatt H., Thompson H. et al., "Pedometer-Measured Physical Activity and Health Behaviors in U.S. Adults." *Medicine and Science in Sports and Exercise* 2010; vol. 42, no. 10 (2010): 1819–1825.

[xxxii] Crichton G.E., Alkerwi A., "Association of Sedentary Behavior Time with Ideal Cardiovascular Health: The ORISCAV-LUX Study." *Public Library of Science One* vol. 9, no. 6 (2014).

[xxxiii] York P., "The Environmental Impacts of Intensive Livestock Operations in Canada." *The Bulletin* vol. 33, no. 1, (May 2013). Retrieved from: http://www.scienceforpeace.ca/the-environmental-impacts-of-intensive-livestock-operations-in-canada#table3.

[xxxiv] Gleick, P.H., *The World's Water Volume 7: The Biennial Report of Freshwater Resources*. (Washington DC: Island Press, 2011)

[xxxv] Pimentel D., Pimentel M., "Sustainability of meat-based and plant-based diets and the environment." *The American Journal of Clinical Nutrition* vol. 78 (September 2003): 660S–663S.

[xxxvi] Bannatyne L., "Where does your recycled bottle go?" *Christian Science Monitor* (September 13, 2005). Retrieved from: http://www.csmonitor.com/2005/0913/p18s02-hfks.html.

[xxxvii] Shimeall E., *Eleanor's Solar Cookbook* (Borrego Springs: Cemese Publishers).

Made in the USA
San Bernardino, CA
27 February 2016